C000060706

Real Golf

120 Useful Ideas for Better Golf and Lower Scores

DAVID GOULD

**Andrews McMeel
Publishing**

Kansas City

02 03 04 05 06 MVP 10 9 8 7 6 5 4 3 2 1

Library of Congress Cataloging-in-Publication Data
Gould, Dave, 1957-
    Real golf : 120 tips for better golf and lower scores / David Gould.
        p. cm.
    ISBN 0-7407-2206-9
        1. Golf. I. Title.

    GV965 .G66 2001
    796.352'3—dc21

                                                2001053870

Book design by Holly Camerlinck

For Caroline, Hannah, and Nathaniel

Contents

Chipping - Club - also p 79

Introduction

Welcome to *Real Golf*. If you agree there are at least 120 ways to bungle a golf shot—or mess up an entire round—you're likely to dive right into the 120 tips and ideas on these pages. They were researched and written to help sharpen the skills (and lower the scores) of the typical dedicated golfer. That's the guy who breaks 90 but not 80, or the woman who makes three or four pars a round and knows she could be making seven or eight.

Each of these people has, at one time or another, walked off the course muttering, "I'm my own worst enemy."

Usually it's because they've let their strengths as a golfer get sabotaged by their weaknesses. On the first par-5 of the day, for example, they might play as follows: Drive in the fairway, six-iron layup to 110 yards, then a skulled pitching wedge into the back bunker, all leading to a three-putt double bogey. They write down a 7 and walk to the next tee thinking: "I usually hit a good drive on this hole, but after that double bogey I'm not sure. What's the use, anyway? I'll probably just flub the wedge shot again . . ." Then they make an uncertain swing.

Think about it: Every shot played on that par-5 hole was fine except the third shot in and the first putt—and anger at the bungled wedge shot was the only reason that first stroke on the green wasn't good enough to prevent a three-putt. So one error brought the whole system down. Ouch, indeed.

Whatever your Achilles heel, it's addressed in this collection of tips. Whichever thread in your golf game is hanging loose and, once pulled, will lead to a complete unraveling, we've got you covered. Even if that loose thread should change, we've still got the solution, just on another page. And think about it: Once you plug the really harmful holes in your game, what fun will it be taking aspects of golf you're already good at and raising them toward mastery?

A book like this—using the expertise of so many different professionals—probably couldn't have been written twenty-five years ago. The knowledge base was nowhere near as wide and deep throughout our teaching profession as it is today. Nor were the psychological aspects of golf as well researched. And the vital links between the equipment in your bag and the type of swing you make simply were not known.

Listen to the clear voices of these teachers and to the specific ideas and instructions they offer. You'll hear first-rate advice on everything from beating the slice to sinking a four-footer, and you'll hear it in the relaxed tones of people who, though they have never met you, know you just the same.

With friends like these, you won't need to worry anymore about being your own worst enemy. Play well, and enjoy every swing.

Chapter 1

Tips for Your Grip and Setup

Grip Tip No. 1: Choose Your Basic Style

Harry Vardon, the turn-of-the-century English pro who was golf's first superstar, made a huge impact on golf by inventing the nine-finger overlap grip. Go to any pro tournament or even country club in America and you'll find 90-plus percent of all golfers taking hold of the club in this manner, in which the little finger of the right hand locks into the notch between the first and second fingers of the left hand. Ironically, neither Jack Nicklaus nor Tiger Woods uses the overlap style. They use the interlocking grip, in which the right pinky actually hooks around and interlocks with the left index finger.

"Nicklaus had small hands," notes Glenn Sowizrol, head professional at White Eagle Golf Club, Naperville, Illinois, "and golfers with small hands tend to be more comfortable with the interlocking grip." As for Tiger? "He's been playing so much golf from such an extremely young age he must never have felt a reason to change from the interlocking method," Sowizrol theorizes.

For new players coming into golf, especially young ones, Sowizrol recommends the ten-finger, or baseball, grip "to get them used to gripping with leverage." Eventually a player can feel somewhat floppy or wristy with the ten-finger grip, or else feel the fingers crowding up on the club handle where the hands come together. The next step would be from baseball-style to interlocking, which brings the club out of the fingers a bit and more into the hands, for stability. A final step would be from interlocking to overlap, or Vardon-style, a transition most male golfers make strictly to look the part of a true golfer.

"Once you've gotten comfortable with a grip style," says Sowizrol, "you've got to move the hands together either to a neutral, slightly strong (turned clockwise on the shaft) or slightly weak (turned counterclockwise) position, and stay there." His best checkpoint for whether your hands are in that proper position? "The club face is square at impact, the back of the left hand is facing the target at impact, and the ball flies reasonably straight." Sounds like an old picture of Harry Vardon.

Plant for Power: Driver Setup Basics

Assuming you take a proper, athletic stance at address for your golf shots, take a moment to check through the setup adjustments recommended for optimum driving by Dave Collins of Shadow Valley Golf Course in Boise, Idaho.

Collins's driver adjustments are simple but specific, as follows:

1. Widen the feet: Your heels should be spread so they are directly under your armpits.
2. The right foot should be set 90 degrees to the ball-target line.
3. Grip pressure should be light.
4. Position the ball off the instep or big toe of your left foot.
5. Tee the ball high; at least half the ball should be over the crown of the driver.
6. Correct posture: head up, no crowding the ball, arms a bit extended.
7. Hands should line up with the inside of the left thigh.
8. The shaft of your driver should be tilted slightly toward the target.
9. Weight should be equally divided between the left and right foot and on the balls of the feet, not out toward the toes or back toward the heels.

That's the turbo-powered preset for great driving. Practice these fundamentals on the driving range, and let fly on the first tee.

Adapt Your Setup to Your Body Type

The golf profession has been influenced in recent years by new ideas relating individual body type to setup and swing mechanics. The point now is to ask: How are you built, where does your power come from, and how should you set up over a golf ball? Chicago-based Jim Suttie pioneered this line of thinking, along with fellow top instructors Mike Adams and T. J.

Tomasi. To get a complete diagnosis of how your basic physique dictates how you should stand and swing, you would have to see a professional familiar with the concept. In general, the connections work like this.

▶ If you have plenty of strength through the chest and shoulders and relatively normal lower-body strength (example: Arnold Palmer), you will generate your golf power from the upper body and swing with a slashing tempo. Thus you'll need a fairly wide stance for stability during the swing. Your grip will be turned somewhat clockwise on the shaft. You are more likely to finish "high" than "low and around."

▶ If you are tall and lean and physically fit (example: Davis Love III) but not bulky in any particular spot, you're most likely to swing on an upright plane with an unhurried tempo that builds speed all the way to impact. Your natural setup is with a narrow-seeming stance (to match your narrow shoulders) and an upright posture.

▶ If you are shorter than average with a normal build, but you still hit it a long way (example: Jeff Sluman), your power probably comes from the speed of your hip and shoulder turn. You're the type of player who tends to stand a little more upright and may appear to be rather far from the ball at address, without much angle between the line of the club shaft and the line established by the left arm. Your stance would tend to be square to the target line, setting up a naturally straight ball flight.

There are probably a dozen or two variations on the body type theory, but golf instructors have taken to the concept enthusiastically because it makes their teaching a little more "real." They don't have to try to fit every student they meet into one perfect model of a swing—something to think about as you ask around about golf instructors in your area.

A Quick Check of Setup Fundamentals

When a professional golf instructor's children become teenagers, there is one parenting skill the golf pro doesn't have to learn: the diplomatic criticism of slumping, slouching posture. Good golf requires decent posture over the ball, which means a golf teacher must constantly nag his students about standing properly over their shots.

Sean Williams, of Springdale Country Club in Canton, North Carolina, is a younger professional who takes an old-school tone of voice when discussing posture and other fundamentals of the setup for a good golf swing. Here is Sean's checklist:

▶ Stand at address with a straight back and spine. Don't curl the shoulders forward and down, but do bow the rear end out. "When your rear end sticks out," explains Williams, "that straightens your back and puts the weight on the balls of your feet, where you want it—unless you want to top the ball or hit it to the right." Williams checks posture by tapping or pressing on students' sternums as they stand at address. "If they maintain their position, that tells me their posture is sound," says Williams. "If they fall back, I know their weight is too much in the heels."

▶ Posture starts at the base and works upward. "Stand like a linebacker in football," says Williams. "Feet should be shoulder-width apart and the shoulders, hips, and feet should all be aligned with each other. They should be on a line that is parallel with the ball-to-target line."

▶ Arms should hang naturally from the shoulders as the club is held at address. "I don't like to see people reaching," says Williams. "As a student is standing at address, I'll tell them to let go of the club and relax. If they're reaching, their arms will swing noticeably back toward their body. That spot where the hands end up is where they should be in the first place."

Sight a Target, Put the Club Down, Then Step In

This is a fairly simple alignment tip, but one all pro-tour players live by. Having worked with many a tournament golfer, Jacques Panet-Raymond, director of the highly successful golf school at Stow Acres Country Club in Stow, Massachusetts, passes it on to his own students religiously.

Jacques's advice is twofold. "First," he says, "pick out your target and your line of flight from squarely behind the ball. When you're in that position, you've got trustworthy binocular vision working in your favor. Before you leave your spot behind the ball, pick out a mark on the grass a few feet in front of your ball that is directly on line to the target."

If you commit to that intermediate target, says Panet-Raymond, your chances of success will be high. Why wouldn't any of us commit to the little mark as a flyover spot? Well, our altered perspective from above the ball at address throws us off. "Standing over the ball, we can't help looking at the target," says Jacques, "and the skew angle it shows us plays havoc with alignment. The average golfer doesn't realize how untrustworthy that view of the target really is."

Along with using the little divot or coloration we picked

out during our preshot, we can complete our commitment to the correct target line by following Panet-Raymond's other basic alignment fundamental: Put the club down in place before we take our stance.

"Every average amateur gets his feet in place first, then sets the club down behind the ball," explains Panet-Raymond. "Every tour pro puts the club down first, in true alignment, then sets his feet and takes his stance." And so, to align like the professionals, you don't need much more than a couple of fundamentals: Pick out an intermediate target from behind the ball and set your wood or iron down with its leading edge perpendicular to that line before you step in and take your stance. Then get comfortable and make a solid, committed swing.

Why Golfers Regrip at the Top and How to Avoid It

Classic golf instruction has long referred with admiration to "the pause at the top" of the backswing. Indeed, that moment of apparent stillness does signify a smooth, unhurried golf swing. But it's also an opportunity for mischief, in the form of either slight wriggling of the club handle or a true letting-go-and-regripping action.

Bill MacLaughlin, professional at Crystal Lake Country Club, Pompano Beach, Florida, says a golfer does this unconsciously, but for the valid reason that he has started out incorrectly at address and/or cupped his wrists on the backswing and is vaguely aware that the only way to get the club face somewhere near a square orientation at impact is to ease off, let it twist, and regrip. "Between whatever you did wrong originally and the centrifugal force that wants to fan the blade open on the backswing, a bit of letting go and regripping can happen pretty easily," says MacLaughlin.

Fundamentals to remember if you feel this might be happening include:

▶ Keep your thumbs slightly to the sides of the handle. "Don't hold the club with the thumbs on top of the shaft, MacLaughlin warns. "Place them so you get a pinching feeling between each thumb and forefinger."

▶ Keep your hands clear of the knob. "Baseball players can actually gain some bat speed and keep control of their bat by sneaking the little finger and even ring finger of their left hand onto the knob of the bat," says MacLaughlin. "Some golfers try this too, but it only leads to trouble." To staunch this cause of regripping, he advises, keep the top half inch of the club handle free.

▶ Have a professional or even a friend check your position at the top. "Ideally, the shaft should be parallel to the ground at the top of the backswing, pointing toward the target," says MacLaughlin, "and the toe of the club should be at a forty-five-degree angle to the ground. Get to that position, and the shots you produce will be good enough that you won't have that feeling you need to regrip." Sounds like classic golf instruction to me.

Chapter 2

How to Add Distance

Educated Hands Crack the Whip for Added Distance

If you aren't getting the yardage you want on your drives, former New England PGA Teacher of the Year Sue Kaffenburgh guarantees there's an answer—and it's right in your hands. You may have often heard that the big muscles of the legs and torso power the golf swing. All well and good, but as Kaffenburgh points out, "The only connection we have with the golf club is our hands." In her experience, hand action more than transmits torso-and-leg power, it actually triggers it. Kaffenburgh's students are shown how "educated hands" provide the extra whip in the swing that makes players of average length into bona fide long drivers.

She wants you to start with a mental image of Indiana Jones and his bullwhip. To make that whip crack with speed, Indy would take the handle back first and then attempt to get the tip of the whip to release first on the way down.

The translation to golf goes like this: Take one of your longer clubs and, on the backswing, let the left hand push the handle (i.e., the top of your club) away first—ahead of the club head, which lags for a foot or so. Once you're at the top of your backswing, move the club downward by again pushing on the handle, only this time you should be intent on getting the club head down to the ball before the handle of the club returns to its original address position. In other words, club head first on the downswing, with the handle (as well as your shoulders, hips, and legs) "losing the race." What you'll feel is your right hand sending the club head directly to the ball with plenty of speed. You will feel your hands produce a new "lever" in your wrists, translating into increased club head speed. The greater momentum you've created will also pull your body to a better finish position, because all your weight will be sent to your left leg as you "chase" the fast-moving club head!

Distance Keys at Point A and Point Z

It's a watchword among teaching pros that the amateur will not play well if multiple swing thoughts are crowding the brain. Dave Collins, a nominee for *Golf Magazine*'s 100 Top Teachers in the U.S. award, has two favorite tips for anyone wishing to add distance without suffering mind static. The beauty of Collins's two shortcuts to length lies in their polar positions along the swing sequence—very beginning and very end.

His tip as you start out involves grip pressure, and it's highly memorable indeed. "Hold the club just as you would hold a tube of toothpaste—with the cap off—if you wanted to make a golf swing without letting any of the toothpaste out of the tube," advises Collins, who is based in Boise, Idaho, at the Shadow Valley Golf Improvement Center. "Tension is a distance blocker, and light grip pressure just about guarantees there will be no excess tension in your swing. You'll swing freely and generate maximum power."

Collins's second swing thought involves every swing's final frame: the finish. "I've never seen a golfer make a good finish without making a good golf swing" is a phrase Collins repeats often. Full power at impact is virtually guaranteed if the finish position is correct. To achieve a sound finish, according to Collins, you first have to get a firm mental lock on your own personal "finish feeling." Once you understand it, take plenty of swings with no thought but getting to that finish. One helpful indicator: hearing a swish sound as your club begins its arc upward from impact. Hear that swish in the early follow-through cycle, power your way to an erect, well-balanced finish, and watch the ball fly. Oh yes, and keep the toothpaste in the tube.

Bigger Drives with a Firm Left Side

Working on driver distance with his students at Kierland Golf Club in Scottsdale, Arizona, teaching professional Ken Carpenter likes to show photos of power pitchers like Roger Clemens or Pedro Martinez just before they release the baseball. These images help him get across the point that, in golf, it helps our driving distance significantly if we can "hit against a firm left side."

What exactly do these photos depict? "They show the chest and shoulders of a Clemens or Martinez squared up to the plate and far ahead of the pitching arm, which is arced back and trailing the body," Carpenter says. The equivalent in golf is the player's rotation of his hips and torso all the way back to the target line while the hands and arms trail the action—all geared up to use the driving force of that body rotation to speed that club head through impact.

The well-known reference to a right-handed golfer's "firm left side" describes the sensation of the body holding its position while the arms and club come barreling down after it. In fact, the body never does pause; but that firm left side, around which the swing's second pivot will occur (the first pivot is around the right leg, on the backswing), is a strobe-quick feeling that confirms a proper, distance-generating sequence of movements.

Swinging for distance via this correct sequence (and developing the firm-left-side sensation) takes practice, and some golfers will be less prone to feel it than others. Seeing your swing on video could help the process. Check the video monitor for that Clemens-Martinez moment, then stop it again a few ticks later, at impact. "Look for your left arm staying solid at impact," advises Carpenter. Then go back to the tee without delay and hit some more drives. If you're making a sound swing that produces impressive yardage, that kinesthetic clue of the left side holding momentarily still (and solid) will become part of your system for feeling powerful, productive swings out on the golf course.

Hit Rockets, Not Pop-Ups, with Right Shoulder Low

Drives that look fine off the club face but "go nowhere" are said to be "skyed." Their cause, according to John Poole of

Chester Valley Golf Club in Malvern, Pennsylvania, is an angle of attack that's too steep. And how is it a golfer gets too steep coming into the ball? "It's usually one of two things," explains Poole, the 2000 Professional of the Year in his PGA section, "a reverse pivot on the backswing (loading up weight on the front foot) or a lowering and a kind of freezing of the head—the old keep-your-head-down rule getting more credence than it deserves."

Poole has a remedy that—if you've never consciously tried it—just might produce one of the sweetest, most solid-feeling sensations you've ever introduced into your swing. And it's simple: Keep the right shoulder down on the backswing.

"Think about getting some shoulder tilt as you move away from the target," advises Poole. "Feel that you're tilting your back shoulder down very slightly as you take the club back. That tilt will naturally put some weight on your back foot, which will give you stability without sacrificing power." (Note: The reverse pivot is a case of gaining a feeling of stability in a way that *does* sacrifice power.)

By tilting the right shoulder down going back, you can position that shoulder behind the ball at the top of the backswing. Poole says the player will almost always "feel that he or she is coming in shallower—like the plane is landing normally on the runway, not dive-bombing." This angle will eliminate skying and cause the ball to fly like a plane taking off, not like a helicopter taking off. Drill this with a wedge: "Practice some short wedge shots without any wrists at all," Poole says. "Swing from waist high to waist high. Hit with your arms and shoulders only—really feel like no wrists are involved." The right-shoulder-low feeling will also occur with this wedge drill. Not only will you be developing muscle memory for your driver swing, you may like the crisp, effortless wedge shots produced by this drill so much you incorporate them right into your short game.

"On the Screws": Old Wisdom That's Ever True

Golfers who collect old clubs are aware that wooden drivers with face inserts originally had those inserts held in place by tiny screws. Thus the expression "on the screws," meaning struck in the exact meaty middle of the driver face. And it was those drives that soared farthest down the fairway. Les Jaco, a highly regarded teacher and club fitter in Jackson, Tennessee, was mentored by a pioneering Tennessee pro named Pat Abbott. The two played golf together often when Abbott was in his sixties and Jaco, a powerful player, was in his golfing prime. Seldom did the younger pro outdrive his elder, moving Jaco to ask Abbott how this was possible.

The reply, according to Jaco, was simply: "I hit the son of a gun on the nose every time." Abbott emphasized center-of-the-face contact more than any teacher Jaco knew, explaining that an off-center hit of just one-half a ball caused significant "distance leakage." Jaco schools his own students in this old wisdom by applying impact tape to the faces of their woods and irons. When a shot flies short, he is usually able to show off-center impact. When a ball rockets off the club face and flies deep toward the target, he typically has an on-center mark to reveal. His advice: Purchase impact tape at a full-service golf shop and spend one practice session out of every few taping your club faces and concentrating on centered hits.

Out on the golf course, check the face of any club hit off the ground. From most lies, there will be a grass imprint that gives you a good idea where on the face you made contact. Correlate that information with the ball flight of the shot. Finally, on a day when you're swinging well and want to make sure not to start analyzing your mechanics, think: *Hit that son of a gun on the nose*, or *On the screws*.

Retime Your Swing to Put Body Ahead of Arms

With the golf swing, it's not just what you do, it's when you do it. This fact of links life plays out most obviously in the timing relationship between body and arms. Walking up and down the practice area at Arrowhead Golf Club in Princeville, Illinois, professional Earl Swanson sees more players getting into trouble by overworking their hands and arms as they underwork their legs and torso. The result of this mistiming is several different forms of lost distance and lost accuracy—mostly pulls and pull-slices.

"The reason it's such a common problem," says Swanson, "is that hands and arms are easier to move and quicker by nature than the big muscles of the body." Swanson starts to work on a problem like this by checking his students for a neutral grip (hands facing one another, the creases between each thumb and forefinger pointing in the same direction) and basically sound alignment at address.

If all that checks out, or once slight corrections are made, he puts them in front of a specially marked mirror on the practice tee and shows them and gets them to feel what it's like when the body moves first and the hands and arms properly follow. "You can do this with any mirror," he says, adding that it would help to lay some white tape vertically down the glass to dramatize this lesson. "The idea is to match the feeling of 'body first' with the image of it, so you can do it later without a mirror."

For a reinforcing drill (which can be done on the golf course while you're waiting to hit, as a handy cue), the player takes his club back to the top, holds it there one beat, then triggers his body turn with a movement of the hips. Only then do the arms follow, which means they deliver the club on a square path with a squaring-up club face. And that's the kind of delivery that spells full distance and reliable accuracy.

Iron Shots Can Sneak Through Wind If You Knock Them Down

"Swing easy, hit hard" was the distance mantra of Julius Boros, who symbolized effortless power on the pro tour of the 1950s and '60s. Golf's knockdown shot, oft discussed but not widely understood, puts the '56 Open champ's seductive slogan into practice. The shot gets its name from the technique a golfer uses to carry his middle-to-long iron 140 to 200 yards into the wind on a gusty day. Ironically, the name also describes what the wind would do to a conventionally played iron shot—"knock it down" short of the yardage that club usually provides.

Aaron Becker, PGA pro on staff at Bent Creek Country Club in Lititz, Pennsylvania, says the knockdown iron shot marks a mature or maturing golfer—someone adding subtlety to his or her game. But he also considers the knockdown a wonderfully easy shot to learn, if not master. Pick up the basics in a few minutes and you can begin experimenting with it right away. Here are the knockdown's basic characteristics:

▶ Flies lower than normal: "A knockdown seven-iron might travel three-iron or four-iron height," says Becker. "Because you swing easier, you give the ball less underspin, which keeps it from rising so high it 'balloons' in the wind."

▶ Skips forward after it lands for one or two hops, then settles nicely.

▶ Flies straight or else draws—will not slice or fade if correctly played.

Here are the knockdown's how-to basics:

▶ Overclub for the yardage. Take one, maybe two clubs more than you would from that distance if playing a standard shot on a calm day.

▶ Choke down on the club an inch to an inch and a half.

▶ Play the ball back in your stance an inch or two.

▶ Due to ball position, feel that your hands are naturally ahead of the ball (ahead = closer to the target) at address. That hands-ahead feeling should repeat itself as you approach impact.

▶ Take the club back slightly low and slightly inside the ball-to-target line. Straight back and high is the wrong recipe for knockdown shots.

▶ Swing about 80 percent of normal force, but keep hands and club head accelerating. Make crisp impact—a thinly struck knockdown shot can fly okay, but hit this shot fat and you're nowhere.

▶ Trust the technique. It may not seem like you're applying enough force to get the ball to the green, but you are. The
key sign is hang time. Your shot keeps traveling through the
wind and reaches its destination via the "low road."

Chapter 3

Make Solid Contact

Better Setup Ends the Misery of Topped Shots

Probably half of all first-tee jitters ever experienced by golfers can be blamed on one dreaded shot—the cold-topped tee ball. Just thinking of it brings winces, especially to players who periodically suffer this fate. Steve Cramer, pro at Crofton Country Club in Crofton, Maryland, traces topping troubles to incorrect posture. The original pose of the body is incorrect, and it gets worse instead of better as the golf swing unfolds.

"What I see most as the root cause of topping and thin shots is the chin tucked too far into the chest at address," explains Cramer. "The likely reason for this is that old keep-your-head-down idea, which tends to cause problems." As the golfer with his chin tucked toward the chest makes a back-swing, relates Cramer, the left shoulder bumps the chin and causes an upward movement of the head. Now the golfer is straightened up and his hand-eye coordination is thrown off.

He has to dip back down to set things right and can't. The club comes through an inch or two due north of the golf ball, and only slight contact is made.

"Eye contact with the ball is what you basically need," Cramer says, "not literally having your head pulled down toward the ball." To banish the topped shot from your repertoire, assume an athletic address position with plenty of space between your chin and your chest.

Fixes on the Fly: John McGuire's "Shoulder Speedup"

This tip comes from the well-stocked "first aid kit" of club professional John McGuire, who hangs his shingle at the Hunting Creek Country Club in Prospect, Kentucky. A veteran head pro who spends his winters competing in Florida, McGuire knows by now to keep a constant eye out for his own personal foible—fat iron shots caused by an overly steep angle of attack. For McGuire, as well as for many students and amateurs he has played with, the source of the error is the tendency to become excessively target-oriented. Focusing on the target is necessary, but if you overfocus on the green or the flagstick you run the risk of forgetting about the golf ball.

Hitting fat is usually just a matter of bringing the leading edge of your club into impact one half to three-fourths inches from the ideal location, says McGuire. The leading edge bumps the turf and then skids the rest of the way to the ball. It's a small error, but it slows the club head enough to drain 15 or 20 percent of the expected force from the shot. When does this really matter? On shots over ponds and lakes, naturally.

The sensation: "My hands are 'outrunning' my shoulders."

The solution: "One simple thought: Keep my shoulders moving through impact."

The tricky part: This little wrinkle in the swing is traceable to the shoulders, which are harder to monitor than the hands. "Usually, we know what's going on with our hands and wrists more than we do the big muscles of our torso and shoulders," says McGuire.

Hit Like a Pro (Not on the Toe)

Formal and informal studies have shown that most uncentered golf hits by most amateurs occur toward the toe—sometimes a little, sometimes a lot. Meanwhile, the wear marks on a tour player's clubs will all be right in the center. Kevin Hamluk, a pro at Minebrook Golf Course, Hackettstown, New Jersey, offers this wisdom on toe hits and how to avoid them.

"Modern club technology tries to offset the toe-hit problem by adding weight to that end of the club," says Hamluk, "but if you miss way out toward the toe, the feeling you'll get will be a wobble through impact." The ball flight, according to Hamluk, will generally be short and fading or slicing to the right.

Causes of the toe hit? "It could be any number of problems, which you would have to check out one by one," he says. "Grip pressure could be too tight (restricting your swing arc), a sway in the swing could cause it, or even posture that is too crouched or too upright." In the irons, toe hitting could be the result of an incorrect shaft flex or a lie angle that doesn't fit the golfer's natural move.

Correcting the problem is a trial-and-error process best done with a professional instructor. A good first step is to buy some impact tape at a golf store, apply it to your club faces at the practice range, and experiment with lighter grip pressure, more athletic posture, and a smoother, more accelerating swing.

Hitting Toward the Heel: An Uncommon Flaw Well Worth Fixing

Teaching professionals generally feel that far more golfers stand too far from the ball than too near, and far more of us miss our shots toward the toe than toward the heel.

But if your clubs show grass stains and wear marks on the heel end of their faces, you're probably hitting unsatisfactory shots and possibly dallying with real disaster. "The big thing with missing far to the heel side is that you're flirting with the dreaded shank," says David Uyehara, who teaches at Desert Willow Golf Club in Henderson, Nevada. Other signs beyond the markings are a "boardy" feel, according to Uyehara, and shots that go somewhat low and off to the right. (Note: On iron shots from fairway and light rough, check the club face right after the shot for an imprint of grass that will reveal where you made impact.)

Causes include standing too close, unconsciously aiming right, or using clubs whose lie angles are incorrect. For the most efficient answer to your heel-hit problem, consult a teaching professional who is also a skilled club fitter and can test you on a flat, plastic surface called a "lie board." Get to him or her before the shanks get to you.

A Tip You're at Liberty to Skip:
Fixing the Shanks

As is the case throughout the entire golfing world, the subject of shanking was brought up reluctantly in these pages—the myth being that mere mention of the syndrome can cause golfers who were going along fine to suddenly begin hitting shots sideways off the hosels of their irons. But silence isn't always golden. Sean Williams, a professional at Springdale Country Club in Canton, North Carolina, was asked to do some diagnostics and how-to that might cure and prevent the shanks.

"It's the worst shot in golf, that's for sure," acknowledges Williams. And what exactly causes it?

"Most players who shank are cutting across the ball with a closed club face," says Williams. "When the hands reach belt-high on the downswing, the toe of the club is out of position but the club shaft is parallel to the ground." From that position, logic dictates, you're basically going to lead into the ball with the club face wide open and nothing but the hosel available to contact the ball. Result: a shot dead sideways, shoulder-high or lower.

Cures for the shanks include strengthening your grip (i.e., turning it clockwise on the handle); swinging back on a flatter plane (i.e., not so upright); and any other fundamental that helps square the club face at address. Williams works with the shank hitter by practicing half-swings with the club face squaring properly. "The first thing to do is calm your nerves about it," says Williams. "It's still just golf—you're not landing 747s in a snowstorm." And, as golf myth and lore teaches us, the shanks, bless 'em, can go away as suddenly as they appeared.

Finish Beautifully and Contact Will Take Care of Itself

In Stephen Covey's best-selling book *The Seven Habits of Highly Effective People*, one of the habits listed is "Begin with the end in mind." For Idaho-based instructor Dave Collins, that thought epitomizes the relationship between solid ball striking and a first-class follow-through and finish. Although the strike of the ball takes place well before the golfer reaches his finish position, Collins, whose learning center is located at Boise's Shadow Valley Golf Course, focuses on the latter in order to achieve the former.

"I've never seen a golfer go to a beautiful finish position without hitting an excellent golf shot," Collins states flatly. Beginning with the end in mind, here are his indicators of an ideal finish position:

▶ Your weight is outside the left foot, more of it toward the heel.

▶ Right foot is up on the toe.

▶ Your thighs are together.

▶ Right hip is more toward the target than the left hip.

▶ Right shoulder is more toward the target than the left shoulder.

▶ You are looking at the target over your right upper arm.

▶ You are standing tall (not arched back in a "reverse C" position).

Collins would add one related observation: The golf ball is flying high, headed right toward the target.

Chapter 4

Fix Slices and Pushes

Misalign and You'll Likely Mis-hit

The problem: full shots that feel dull at impact and drift or curve to the right of the target, covering shorter distances than expected. The swing flaw: There isn't one—or there may not be, explains Belmont Country Club director of golf John Fields. The whole problem could be your setup and alignment, skewed to the left.

"The way you prove this is to observe the shots that you do hit well and track whether they all end up left of the target. If you're out there 160 or 170 yards from the green saying, 'Shoot, I pulled it!' but secretly you're a little happy that you at least hit one on the screws," says Fields, "that's the giveaway."

Why the problem occurs: Standing at address for a golf shot is visually awkward. Your view of the target line is skewed by the natural tilt of your head. The result is a visual picture that isn't truly binocular—the way it is when you are standing behind the ball lining up your shot. "Often when you see a golfer fidget with his stance at address, it's the optical problem kicking in," says Fields. "The view he had from behind the ball is being challenged by the view he has standing over it. The stance starts to open up because the eyes want that binocular view back." With the body aligned left, the club will either "follow the body" and hit what amounts to a pull, or else the club will swing away from the hip-and-shoulder line and arrive at impact with the club face open, causing a weak fade.

Avoiding the problem: "First of all, trust your brain's ability to 'remember' the ball-to-target line it locked onto when you stood behind the ball getting ready," advises Fields. "Once you're in your stance, do what it takes to get comfortable, but listen to that little voice that's telling you to realign." Having extra trouble with this? Set the blade down immediately behind the ball, establishing a T that's composed of the target line and the leading edge of the club. Make your final adjustments without erasing that T. Then, as Fields exhorts his own students, "Just trust in your setup and make a great swing."

Proven Slice Beaters: Proper Shoulder Turn and Coil

It's said that tension and tightness are destructive to the golf swing, but that mostly relates to overly tight grip pressure and a resulting lockup of the hands and arms. Award-winning teacher Rick Sayers, of Anchorage Golf Club in Alaska, reminds us that a sound swing will create a bit of momentary and productive tension—the coiled feeling we get through the upper torso when we complete a proper shoulder turn.

Average golfers who are slicing repeatedly should seriously check out their coil and shoulder turn, says Sayers. "Take a series of practice backswings and notice whether you're actually turning away from the ball or just lifting the club handle up and keeping it more or less in front of you. That's not making a proper takeaway and coil." Other indicators, according to Sayers, are having your back to the target at the top of the backswing and a noticeable feeling of torque in the upper body. "By the time your hands are belt-high on the takeaway," he says, "shoulder turn should have begun and you should start to feel it happening."

If you have access to a mirror at your practice range, spend a few minutes checking these positions visually as well as through feel. "As a takeaway swing thought, you might think of yourself handing a basketball to a person standing to your right," says Sayers. Finally, hold that coiled, slice-preventing backswing long enough in practice to check the club head position: it should be pointing at the target with the toe of the club pointing toward the ground.

A Follow-Through Tip from One of the Finest

As it would in most athletic movements, the full and flowing follow-through in the golf swing virtually guarantees success. We all know it, but with so much else to think about we too often fail to finish our swings.

Davis Love Jr., father of the tour star Davis Love III, was a brilliant teaching professional who died tragically in the crash of a small plane. His renowned teaching skills included many an impromptu, midround cue or memory key that could get a

⌐ g golfer back in form. During this writer's own slice-plagued round with Davis in the mid-1980s, Love took a tee from his pocket and slid it into the vent hole in the grip cap of the most recently misswung club.

"Don't do anything different," he asked, "just make that tee point away straight out from your left ear when you've finished the swing." The next swing, wonder of wonders, ended in a full follow-through, and the ball went straight as a string. Next time you find yourself quitting early on your swing and hitting weak slices, stick a tee in your grip cap and think of Davis Love Jr.'s advice.

Weak and Leaky Long Irons? Take Out Tension to Add Power

The 170-plus-yard iron shot is among the toughest in golf to hit with authority. According to Dave Bobber, of Trappers Turn Golf Club in Wisconsin Dells, Wisconsin, most golfers consider the least satisfactory shot with a three-iron, four-iron, or even five-iron to be a combination push-fade.

"In general it's a dead-feeling shot," says Bobber. "You get that wounded duck flight that's low and leaks to the right, landing well short of the target."

His suggestions for correcting this are mostly physical, but mental as well. "First, check out the equipment, especially the shaft flex," says Bobber. The simplest way to this is to raid the demo rack at a local driving range or go through a club-fitting session with a custom fitter. "It's common for irons to be too stiff-shafted for the amateur golfer using them," says Bobber. In evaluating other clubs or your own, look on the face for signs of off-center impact. Hits on the center should produce fairly satisfactory ball flight. If they don't, you may indeed need an equipment change.

Whenever you practice long irons, be aware of your grip pressure. "Tension in the wrists and hands is a major cause of the weak, faded iron shot," says Bobber. Use a personal grip-tension scale, from 1 to 5, with 5 being the most grip pressure and 1 the least. Hit practice balls working your way toward the 1 setting. "There's a tempo tip you can also use to fix this problem," says Bobber, "with the idea being that you 'borrow' the tempo and pace of your favorite club—the seven-iron or whatever—and use that same feeling for the longer club that's giving you trouble." Hit the favorite club, groove that tempo, then hit the longer club. Repeat this little drill four or five times, and you may see your long iron shots straightening out and flying a suitable distance.

Don't Slice It—Learn the Controlled Fade

Years of experience on the lesson tee has taught Jeff Minton something he would like to teach all average golfers—if they're ready for it: "The straight golf shot is a myth." According to Minton, most golfers confuse control of their shots and delivery of the ball to an intended target as "hitting it straight." What really happens in most good shots, Minton explains, is that the ball goes on a slightly curving flight from where it lies to (hopefully) a selected spot on the fairway or green. "To try and hit a round little golf ball straight is crazy," says Minton, who teaches at the Golf Club at Newcastle in Newcastle, Washington. "Since most right-handers work their ball from left to right, the real trick is to learn the controlled fade."

Here's how:

Aim your feet, hips, and shoulders slightly left of the target line. Swing on a consistent path (i.e., no Jim Furyk Loop) that matches the lines of your body at setup. Let the club strike the ball as flush as possible with the head traveling slightly down that left-of-target-line track. Look for a ball flight that is initially straight, then begins working to the right toward the top of the trajectory.

One other point: "A shot that fades will travel a little shorter than a shot that draws," says Minton. "If you play the controlled fade, expect to take one more club than someone of roughly equal strength who plays a slight draw."

When practicing this shot, start with a seven- or eight-iron and get your shots fading subtly. This will give you the feel of the swing path and impact position that then carries over to your longer clubs.

An Underhanded Remedy for
Slice-Prone "Overhand" Swingers

One of the fundamental truths of the golf swing for Jim Roeder is that most golfers swing overhand, not underhand, as they ought to. The result is a world full of slicers. For Roeder, based at Emerald Lakes Golf Centre in Elk Grove, California, the golf-swing model from another sport would be a discus thrower, not a baseball pitcher. Unless, of course, that baseball pitcher were a submariner, the type who dropped his right shoulder way low and nearly scraped the mound with his hand delivering the pitch.

To switch yourself from a slice-prone, power-deficient "overhand" golfer to a match-winning underhander, says Roeder, observe the following fundamentals:

▶ Take the club back along the target line; don't let the hands and club head drift inward from that line.

▶ Start your downswing with your lower body leading. "The most obvious sign of the overhand swing problem is starting the downswing with the upper body—the shoulders, mainly," says Roeder. "Think about working your right shoulder under."

▶ Continue this action by feeling the lower body, not the upper body, deliver your body weight to your left side. "Hitting practice shots with these thoughts in mind should make a lot of other corrections happen automatically," Roeder says. "Once you get rid of that violent shoulder motion toward the ball, you'll feel a better release of the wrists and an easier motion toward the full finish position."

As you might expect, Roeder suggests tossing a ball underhand repeatedly before beginning a practice session. That simple exercise will help alert the "golf section" of the brain to that all-important underhand feeling.

The "Post Up" Move Means Square Impact and No Slices

With the help of a deceptively simple practice aid, the humble "impact bag," Barry Troiano of Westchester Country Club in Harrison, New York, gets chronic slicers to a "posted up" finish position that straightens out their slice in surprisingly short order. You can purchase a commercially made impact bag from golf stores or Web sites, or you can make one.

Start with a fifteen-pound bag of sand and wrap it in thick foam insulation. Lightly wrap a few layers of duct tape around it to keep the foam in place. Then find a heavy canvas or thick vinyl bag big enough to hold a beach ball. Place the wrapped bag of sand in the canvas bag and tie it off securely. Keep your impact bag in the trunk of your car with your golf clubs and bring it to the range with you.

"Hitting the side of the bag and working on what I call the post-up move is really effective with someone who's slicing," says Troiano. "We start by getting the golfer to make some practice swings, feeling the weight on his feet move from equal to heavy on the right foot (during the backswing) to fully on the left foot at the finish." That fully weighted left side is the "post up" feeling, and with it comes a full shoulder turn around to the left, a poised torso facing the target, and a comfortable sense of balance that allows the finish to be held indefinitely—not to mention powerful, straight golf shots.

Once this feeling is identified in practice swings, Troiano has the slice-fighting golfer make several swings at the impact bag. "You don't make a big, long swing and you don't have to hit the bag hard at all," says Troiano. After these swings at the bag, step up and swing full at the golf ball. "No mechanical thoughts are needed," says Troiano, "just that sense of getting posted up, with the swing comfortably completed." Unlike some antislice therapies, this concept very often works immediately. And shrewd golfers who try it once or twice on the Westchester range waste no time getting an impact bag of their own.

Chapter 5

Fix Hooks
and Pulls

No Shot Like the High Draw, Until It
Starts to Over Turnover

One of the most satisfying ball flights in all of golf is the medium to high draw—the ball that starts out just right of the intended landing area, then curves slightly to the left at its apogee, falling on a subtle slant toward the target. "C'mon, baby," the player who hits this shot will say as it makes its climb, "turn over, now."

If you live by this shot, you can sometimes suffer with its unintended consequences as well. We're talking about a streak of drives and low-iron or middle-iron shots that turn over an excessive amount, landing in the left rough (for a righty golfer), the left water, or left woods. Dave Johnson of Rancho Canada Golf Club in Carmel, California, offers helpful advice to victims of the "over turnover" shot. He starts it out by referring to one of golf's most universal fundamentals.

"When a high, soft draw turns into a high hook," Johnson inquires, "what is happening with the back of the player's left hand at impact? Is it rolling too far to the left as impact is taking place? That's the first factor to check out."

Indeed, if this problem crops up midround, Johnson would encourage the player experiencing it to focus solely on the back of the left hand during impact and plug in a swing thought that will keep that part of the anatomy facing either toward the target or slightly right of it. On the practice range, he would get into several more fundamentals, including setup (Is the stance too closed?); grip (Have the hands rotated too far clockwise, to an overly "strong" position?); and backswing (have the wrists cocked too early, which might cause an early uncocking on the downswing?).

Another possible cause of this hooking action is a right elbow that gets tucked into the rib region too early in the downswing. It's an interesting ball-flight problem, in Johnson's view. The basic high draw being a very desirable shot, its corruption into a high, hard hook is usually caused by a sound swing fundamental becoming, in his words, "overcooked."

Big- and Small-Muscle Tips to Help Hookers

Helping his hook-prone members at Ridgewood Golf Club with their basic swing flaw comes naturally to Bill Adams, head pro at the Ridgewood, New Jersey, club. Turns out Adams is a hooker himself.

"It's rare that I'm not doing something to try and keep the overly right-to-left shot out of my own game," admits Adams.

"Like a lot of people who hit a natural hook, I have fast hands through impact. My hips lose the race, the club face closes, and the ball swings hard left."

Adams suggests the following adjustments for hookers looking to straighten out their ball flight:

▶ Stand up out of the shot sooner. "People who hit slices are often told it's because they didn't stay down on the shot through impact—they straightened up too early. But if you hook it you may have taken that positive fundamental of staying down through impact and overdone it." Try coming out of the shot sooner, says Adams, "just like you would if you were hitting into a low sun and you were worried you wouldn't be able to see where your ball went."

▶ Think of the toe and heel of your club face racing into impact and finishing in a tie. "For most people who hook, the toe of the club head gets to the ball sooner than the heel, so get a clear picture of the heel keeping pace with the toe." It also helps, he says, to imagine the club face facing the sky as the club reaches belt-height on the follow-through.

As a drill, Adams suggests an idea that is so classic it may even sound a little primitive: "Go to the range and try hitting fifty slices in a row." Even more effective for Adams is to chip fifty or a hundred practice balls with a nine-iron, keeping close visual track of the club face and grooving the feeling of a square face angle. "Chipping acts like a lab experiment that isolates the problem," he says. "You're making a small, relatively slow swing where you're controlling the club face at impact. You can see it and feel it, which allows you to program in a feel that translates to full shots with the woods and irons." If all else fails, he says, tweak your grip. "Take hold of the club with more grip pressure in your left hand than your right," suggests Adams. "Give yourself the feeling that the right hand is along for the ride."

The Pull-Fade Is a Shot You Can Live With (Here's How)

For every ten students who step on the lesson tee with Chris Seabock of Briarwood Golf Club in Ankeny, Iowa, at least one or two are habitual hitters of the pull-fade. According to Seabock, this type of ball flight doesn't earn style points, but it's a shot pattern golfers can be successful with if they understand its elements and can produce it efficiently. Here are some questions Seabock would ask to help you evaluate and repeat the pull-fade shot.

1. Does it reach a reasonably high trajectory for the club being used? "A ball that starts left of the target line and fades right is playable in most conditions," says Seabock, "but if you're hitting it on a low line and never getting reasonable height, it will set you up for trouble rather than success."

2. How far left does it start and how far right does it land? "If you're keeping this shot over the fairway or the first cut of rough as it starts out and getting it to land in the fairway or the first cut of rough on the opposite side, that's a workable shot," he says. "If it's outside those parameters it's not trustworthy."

3. How often do you start the shot out to the left (for a right-handed player) and then see it stay left, or worse, hook to the far left? That's what TV commentator

Johnny Miller refers to as the "dreaded double-cross," and it's a condition Seabock would like to see happen fewer than two or three times a round. "The pull-fade is caused by a player aligning off the target line and then not releasing or unhinging his wrists and hands through impact," Seabock explains. "Whenever this player does release through impact, the ball will go a long way off line and into trouble."

If this is happening during preround warmup, Seabock advises taking some swings with the thought of "holding on" through impact. A short series of practice shots with this idea in mind should return the "educated block" that produces a consistent pull-fade.

Chapter 6

Tempo, Timing, and Rhythm

Tempo Tips for Out-of-Synch Golfers

A major cause of tempo deficiencies in average golfers can be found in, well, books like this. We're talking about golf swing mechanics, a subject on which vast amounts of thinking, discussing, and researching have been done. In the view of professionals like Dave Collins—himself a swing mechanics expert who could speak ad infinitum about positions and angles—the sheer amount of mechanics information drowns out the importance of tempo. You have to counter this, he says, by always coming back to tempo and rhythm.

"Make a rule for yourself to include tempo in your warmups and practice," Collins advises. "The feeling of your swing's pace and timing and overall shape should get its share of time and attention." Methods for doing this include:

▶ Swinging with your eyes closed

▶ Feeling that your swing is a circle and that its rounded shape naturally gives it a flowing motion

▶ Understanding what sort of tempo you have, how your golf swing's momentum is maintained, and where it speeds up and slacks off

▶ Knowing the obstacles to maintaining your natural tempo. "Pressure is the big obstacle—it speeds you up without you knowing it," says Collins.

One way to simplify these questions, Collins feels, is to work on establishing your smooth tempo in the backswing and evaluating it according to how full, upright, and in balance you finish. The part in between, which is the business portion of your swing, should take care of itself. "That feeling of where you want to be at your finish is a great guidepost," he promises.

Take Tempo Cues from Other Sports

The rise of robustly athletic golfers like Tiger Woods and David Duval have, one hopes, done away with the irritating question "Is golf a sport?" The answer is an emphatic yes, and for instructor Chuck Wike, that truth brings to light some helpful comparisons. In his view, the movements we make in playing other sports can greatly enhance our golf swing, particularly in areas like timing and tempo.

"Any golfer who also plays basketball and has a nice fifteen-foot jump shot has a wonderful point of comparison for the rhythm and tempo of his golf swing," claims Wike, proprietor of the Classic Swing Golf School in Surfside Beach, South Carolina. Likewise, a devoted swimmer who can't stop rushing his downswing would do well to dive in a pool and execute a proper breast stroke for several laps. It is similar to a proper golf swing in that you can't possibly rush the motion, or cheat on the extension of your arms, without losing power dramatically.

"There are huge correlations between, say, the tennis stroke, passing a football, and swinging the golf club," Wike says. "Each of them has a point in which you have to make one body motion wait until another motion is completed." Getting quick with your golf swing? Leave the practice tee and go shoot jump shots for thirty minutes. When you come back, the timing and tempo of a solid golf swing may have magically returned.

Great Tempo Through the Round

Standing with your driver and a bucket of balls on the practice range and working your way into a Sam Snead–like swing tempo is a helpful exercise. Just remember, advises teaching pro Charley Estes, that "the tempo for each shot might be a little different" than that flowing Snead-style swing you made while warming up with your driver.

"You never want to rush a swing or 'get quick,'" concedes Estes, who is based at New Sandy Burr Golf Course in Wayland, Massachusetts. "But if you have to play a punch shot from the fairway or a recovery from deep rough, you'll need a different pace to your swing to do it." Think of there being "different flavors" of tempo, Estes advises, with the general rule that you must set up in balance and maintain balance through the swing.

The longer the shot and the better the lie, the more your swing tempo will resemble the flowing Snead model. "Seymour Dunn taught his students to swing a string with a weight on the end," Estes points out. "Harvey Penick told students to imagine they were swinging a half-full pail of water, and they didn't want to spill a drop."

These cues should help you establish your basic rhythm and tempo at the start of the day. When you have to alter that to suit a particular lie (a lazy lob shot, for example, might demand an even slower tempo than you use with a driver), be sure to "rehearse the previous swing tempo out of your system." Remember, too, that nervousness or anxiousness is the biggest enemy of correct tempo. "Visualize every swing and every shot before you play it," says Estes. "While you're doing that, tell yourself: 'See it, feel it, trust it.' Once you're over the ball knowing what you want to do, say 'Trust it' one last time." Tempo alters slightly from shot to shot, but staying calm will prevent the really big tempo mistakes from fouling up your golf game.

One Teacher's Unconventional— but Musical—Route to Better Golf

Several years ago, the iconoclastic golf coach Chuck Hogan (whose students include successful tour pros such as Peter Jacobsen) told a group of fellow instructors at a clinic about a game-improvement technique he had used successfully on students who were musically inclined and didn't mind experimental learning concepts.

Hogan's little system works like this: Sometime during a lesson series, the golfer selects a CD of music he not only loves but also considers fairly conducive to golf (for example, a jazz ballad might be better than heavy metal). Then they match it to a visual. "The instructor and the student screen some videotape of a successful lesson, looking for a series of swings that are among the student's best," explains Hogan. Using a digital editing machine, they dub a thirty-minute, repeating sequence of these four or five excellent swings, with the song selected by the student as musical background.

"Before the golfer goes to the golf course for his nine o'clock tee time," says Hogan, "he loads this video or DVD in the player in his den and watches it while he goes through his morning stretching. Then he gets in his car with the CD and listens to that same music as he drives to the course. By the time he's ready to play, his brain is so visually and aurally connected to those beautiful golf swings, he can't help but play to the top of his capabilities."

As a game-improvement technique, it's a little unconventional to apply universally, but Hogan certainly has no doubts about its merit. When he finished explaining it to his audience, he paused a moment, then added, only half-kiddingly, "Why did I just tell you all this idea? It's too great to give away free."

Tempo Tips for Less Powerful Swingers

Many in the golf instruction ranks are still talking about an article that ran in *Golf Digest* several years ago linking swing tempo to the type of shaft a golfer should use. The story was titled "It's Not How Fast You Swing, It's How You Swing Fast," and it showed, for example, that a 260-yard driver like Nick Price actually needed a stiffer shaft than a 300-yard driver like John Daly—all because of tempo and the various points during the swing when energy gets stored in the shaft (called "loading") and released ("unloading").

Brian Natzel, a professional at Garland Resort in Gaylord, Michigan, refers to these concepts when he teaches his younger, older, and female students about swing tempo. "The idea is to have your optimum combination of speed and control occurring at the impact segment of your swing," says Natzel.

For the tall junior or the woman player, this thought can be especially helpful. What to look for? The feeling of slow club head delivery and the overall appearance that you are more unraveling than exploding through impact. To address the problem, Natzel suggests a reduced amount of hip rotation going back. "Women golfers rely for power on flexibility and the ability to turn back a long way," he explains. "That's fine, but you can overdo it. The culprit is the hips, and they should turn less if the swing is leaking energy through impact."

Try placing a tee in the ground about four or five feet behind the ball, on an extension of the ball-to-target line, and be sure not to let your belt buckle turn farther back than that tee. "You don't have to swing hard to hit the ball fairly far," Natzel notes, "but you do have to create some backswing coil and then uncoil at the right time coming through."

Chapter 7

Shots from Rough and Fairway

How to Play from a Downhill Fairway Lie

Pretty pictures of golf holes show the landscape twisting, rising and falling in photogenic fashion. Then we hit a big tee shot on one of these holes and find ourselves with a downhill lie in the fairway. At that point, pretty turns into pretty tough. A professional from the rolling fairways of River Pointe Golf Club in Albany, Georgia, Gary Clark, lays out the adjustments we need to succeed from this type of lie.

"The problem for mid- to high-handicappers is that they tilt back against the slope," says Clark, "when they should be tilting with it." Step by step, we should try the following:

1. Set up with the left shoulder lower than the right, and with our feet adjusted to allow for that tilt and still maintain balance. (Note: a little extra weight goes on the front foot.)

2. Take one or two clubs more than we would normally hit from this distance on a level lie.

3. Make a backswing slightly more upright than usual (keeping extra weight on the forward foot encourages this), and focus on hitting down on the ball.

If it seems appropriate, we can also choke down slightly on the club, and we should feel free to make a swing that finishes with the left foot coming unplanted and "stepping over," in the style of Gary Player. If we hit it solidly, Clark says, the ball will fly lower and run more. Hopefully, we can count on the architect who designed this rolling fairway to keep the front of the green clear of hazards and allow our lower-flying, longer-rolling ball to bounce up onto the green.

Only Slight Adjustments Needed on Uphill Fairway Lies

Like the sidehill fairway lie in which the ball is above your feet, the uphill fairway lie is a welcome variation on dead level—a lie you can get comfortable over and expect reasonable success from.

Damon Anderson, of the Southwind Golf Club in Garden City, Kansas, has a few adjustments he recommends you employ when playing from the fairway with an uphill (but laterally level) lie. The ball flight on a well-struck shot from this lie will be recognizable, he begins. "It should hang in the air longer and fly a little shorter," explains Anderson. "Where you'd use a seven-iron from a level lie at the given yardage, the uphill lie will call for a six-iron."

But even with the extra club, you should play aggressively, according to Anderson. "The ball will fly high and land soft," he says. "These shots don't generally get away from you." As for technique, use the same ball position you would on a level lie, swing on a slightly more upright plane, and think about hitting the bottom of the back of the ball. More thin hits result from this type of lie than fat hits. As for direction, when in doubt, aim a little left, as the uphill fairway lie will sometimes influence your shot a bit right of where you want it to go.

The "Launching Pad" Effect: Ball-Above-the-Feet Fairway Lie

Uneven fairway lies—long the norm on British and Irish courses—are becoming more common at America's country clubs and public courses. These uneven lies come in four varieties: uphill, downhill, ball below the feet, and ball above the feet. Commenting on the latter, Bob Lennon, of Blue Heron Pines Golf Club in Cologne, New Jersey (and the *Golf Digest* Schools instruction staff) makes a wry but true comment:

"For the high-handicap golfer," Lennon observes, "a lie with the ball above his feet causes him to hit the greatest golf shots of his life." Why is that? For once (in reaction to the ball's ankle-high coordinates), this player's swing path isn't just up and down but *around* as well, which means his hands and wrists are much more likely to unhinge or "release" through impact. Those forces cause a big, straight golf shot that takes off as though fired from a launching pad.

Bearing this bit of golf magic in mind, here is how to handle your typical ball-above-the-feet lie:

▶ Choke down on the club a comfortable amount—enough so you won't hit the shot fat but not so much that you'll be straining or lunging to make contact.

▶ Make practice swings on the plane you'll be using to hit the shot. Feel your balance staying away from your heels and feel the club going naturally more "around" than "up and down."

▶ Expect the ball to go naturally left of where you're aligned; adjust by aiming slightly right of your target.

▶ Allow the club to release and move around you to a full follow-through, but don't encourage this with "active hands." Let it happen naturally.

▶ If you're having to cover a long distance and have taken out a low iron or lofted wood, bear in mind that a fairly major directional error ("30 or 40 yards left is possible," says Lennon) could result even if your strike of the ball is only moderately off your desired face angle and club-path angle. That's simply because your shot is carrying a long distance, thus magnifying the error at impact.

"For a severe ball-above-the-feet lie," says Lennon, "you may not be able to execute a 180- to 220-yard shot reliably at all. In those situations, you have to consciously 'hang on' through impact and really block the releasing action of your wrists and the club head." Given how unpredictable a shot like this can be, Lennon's advice is to "take a six-iron and lay up." Then finish the hole with a chip-and-putt for par.

The "Hanging Lie": Ball Below Your Feet

If an uneven lie with the golf ball above your feet is a "launch pad" prone to turbocharging the average golfer's shot, its opposite—ball-below-the-feet—is a condition in which swing power is often thwarted. Also known as a "hanging lie," the fairway lie with the ball on a level some two to four inches below your spikes is a shot to be cautious with.

Walter Hix III of Wildhawk Golf Club in Sacramento, California, says, "Most tour pros would be delighted to play a medium to long iron from a below-the-feet lie and be able to play their next stroke with a putter."

Here is Hix's prescription for us non–tour players faced with an uneven lie of this type.

▶ Take one extra club than the yardage suggests.

▶ Make practice swings on ground contoured to match your actual stance and lie. Find where your swing bottoms out and adjust your ball position accordingly.

▶ Aim left, and expect the ball to go right.

▶ Keep the swing simple: Focus on maintaining balance and avoid quickness in the backswing, which will move you off your center of balance and cause a significant mis-hit.

Finish this shot more "up" than "around." And if the ball settles on the green—even 50 feet from the hole—declare victory and march onward.

The Shot from Hardpan: Not All That Hard

Modern course grooming is on its way to making hardpan lies as common as cottonseed hull greens. In the meantime, you will still encounter areas of very firm, dry, compacted clay soil, especially in the Southwest or at courses where the golf-cart paths aren't paved. Troy Dickson, of Forest Creek Golf

Club in Round Rock, Texas, explains how hardpan lies react and how to handle them like a pro.

"The advantage of a hardpan lie is that there's nothing specifically hindering the club head as it makes contact," says Dickson. "The challenge is that you've got to nip the ball, not try to slide into it from an inch or two behind. If you do that, the club head will skid, slowing down and possibly twisting before impact."

Position the ball forward in your stance on a hardpan lie, counsels Dickson, and take one less club if there's serious trouble just beyond your target area. "You'll be hitting the shot a little bit thin, and it could come out low and hot," Dickson explains. Make a normal length swing and focus on sweeping into the ball, not attacking steeply downward on it. Despite this shallow angle of approach, you're still trying to pinch the ball off the surface, not plow into it from behind.

Due to the unyielding nature of the hardpan, there could be a "flinch factor," Dickson points out. He advises any golfer who fears injury and might flinch or quit on a hardpan shot to take a wedge and chip it to the fairway rather than attempting a lengthy shot to the green.

The Long Shot from Fairway Grass That's Supershort

There is an ever-evolving relationship that exists among golf courses, golf swings, and golf equipment. Change and progress occurs in one sector, then the other two sectors cycle along with their own advancements. A prime example is the fairway mower height used on modern golf courses. It's surely a sign of great grooming to have your fairway turf cut as short as a top-notch green would have been cut twenty-five years ago. On the other hand, how is an average player going to take a big swing and make solid contact from 220 yards when there's basically no grass beneath his ball to tee it up a bit, only hard ground with a moss-thin coating?

The problem has been addressed via new equipment, observes Gary Clark, a pro at River Pointe Golf Club in Albany, Georgia, but the advantage is still with the tight fairways.

"You can deal with this kind of lie by using either a metal wood with a lot of loft, one of the hybrid 'driving irons' companies are making, or with one of the new low-profile fairway woods," Clark says. At his club, the members go more for conventional head size but extra loft, "in the seven-wood to nine-wood range," reports Clark. Using a club of this type, Clark has them:

▶ choke down slightly if it provides an extra degree of confidence

▶ play the ball slightly forward in the stance

▶ swing full, but in control, focusing on square contact with the back of the ball

They are also encouraged to play the ball more toward the middle of the stance if their basic shot is right to left and follows a slightly low trajectory. "That way they'll get a lot of run and travel a good distance toward the green," he says. "Especially for seniors, this type of situation calls for common sense and maybe conservative strategy. It's a tough shot to hit pure, so the goal is to avoid topping or hitting the shot fat. Decent contact will get you down the fairway and usually in good shape for a shorter pitch to the green."

An Average Golfer's Guide to the Flyer Lie

Most of what average players know about so-called flyer lies they hear from television broadcasters who are describing how tour pros grapple with these shots. We shouldn't, according to the experts, carry too much of that information to our own games. "The middle- to high-handicapper won't have the same experience with flyer lies as a tour pro," says Keith Doshier, of the Links at Pasa Robles, in Pasa Robles, California. "Average golfers lack the club-head speed to propel a ball that is sitting down slightly in light or moderate rough on the tour pro's trajectory," he says. As a result, we won't end up hitting six-iron shots that fly our normal six-iron distance, land "hot," and skip through the green—which is the problematic outcome faced by touring pros.

For us, the guide to handling flyer lies is as follows:

▶ We first evaluate the amount (and density) of grass the ball is nesting in. If half or more of the ball is down in the grass, we will probably have to hit a layup shot with an eight-iron, nine-iron, or wedge.

▶ If two-thirds or more of the ball is showing, we can play a fairly normal approach shot, but we may need one extra club than we would need from this distance on the fairway. "If there's room to land the ball and let it skip a couple of times onto the green," says Doshier, "you may not need to take an extra club. The flyer shot goes shorter in the air than a fairway shot with the same iron, but it's spinning less, so it will tend to run more." If there's water fronting the green, consider a safety shot onto some friendly patch of fairway.

▶ Certain technical adjustments are called for. "Use your normal swing, but play the ball back in your stance a bit," advises Doshier. "That way you'll minimize the amount of grass slowing your club down and cushioning impact." This adjustment may cause your ball flight to be a little lower.

These tips are most applicable when the club in question is a four-, five-, six- or seven-iron. More lofted irons will be minimally affected by the flyer lie, and fairway woods will handle the grassy conditions with significantly less effect on the shot's distance and trajectory.

Chapter 8

Standard Bunker Shots

Back to Bunker Basics with the Dollar Bill Drill

Ever get in a "bunker slump"? It's a devilish bit of golf torture that can strike experienced players and get them feeling paranoid about landing in any "cat box" on the course, even the shallow ones that offer plenty of landing space between bunker edge and green.

For help with this basic golf stroke, we turn to Ed Hoard, of Athens Country Club in Athens, Georgia. This former PGA Professional of the Year begins by reminding the bunker-slumping player of a simple, sane reality: You're not hitting a golf ball to escape the bunker, "you're just moving sand." It's against the rules (and Hoard is a renowned rules expert whom you may have seen officiating play during the PGA Championship) to practice moving sand during a round, so get back in the swing of your basic bunker play by "advancing sand" in a practice bunker—don't even use a ball at first, advises Hoard.

"It may help to think of it as a divot of sand," Ed offers. "I have my students do this a half-dozen times to get comfortable, then put a dollar bill down on the sand, with a golf ball on top of President Washington's face. Then I have them make a swing with the idea of contacting the sand at the front edge of the dollar bill. They find they can advance the dollar bill (on a calm day) eight to 12 feet, and the ball pops out cleanly without them even thinking about it."

Hoard restates the fundamentals as his golfers continue this drill. Your setup should position the ball even with your own center of balance, perhaps your sternum. The swing is relaxed and even-tempo but with no deceleration and a full follow-through. The furthest point of entry from the ball is one-half the length of a dollar bill, but it could be shorter, depending on conditions. Above all, says Hoard, don't get oversold on the idea of *digging* the ball out.

"I come back to that idea of a divot," says Hoard, "and it's a divot that's only a half-inch to an inch deep at its deepest point." He has another image to suggest, this one involving water. "Think of kids in a swimming pool having a little water fight," he suggests. "If they want to advance a plume of water at the other kid, they bring the heel of their hand in on a shallow angle, not a steep one. The way you want to move that sand to hit a bunker shot is just like the way kids in a pool send water at each other." Sounds like advice that could help you win a dollar bill or two out on the golf course.

Miss the Head Cover to Land Sand Shots on Quick, Small Greens

Average golfers tend to live by the rule that "any out's a good out" from greenside bunkers, but on courses with small, fast greens (lots of Donald Ross designs come to mind), you may want to raise the bar a bit higher. That means lofting your golf ball a little higher—higher than what it takes to get it over the lip, that is. Jim Fitzgerald, head pro at the Chevy Chase Club in Bethesda, Maryland, offers these fundamentals for golfers with serious up-and-down ambitions.

"To produce this shot," explains Fitzgerald, "you have to hinge your wrists early and swing your arms up on the backswing, rather than straight back and inside. That's the backswing shape you need to create a steep angle of attack to the ball," which will land it softly and make it settle quickly.

With your stance and club face open to the target line, make your takeaway and backswing, Fitzgerald advises, with an imaginary head cover lying about 12 inches behind the ball. "If you practice this way, then mentally place that head cover a foot or so behind the ball," he says, "you will naturally make the right-shaped backswing and forward swing. It's a nice shortcut for learning how to bring the club in closer to the ball," which is what you want in this greenside bunker scenario. At first, you may need to practice this with the head cover 14 or 16 inches behind the ball, but with repetitions you'll be able to move it in closer.

From Uphill Bunker Lies, Set Up on a Slight Tilt and Swing Away

The greenside bunker shot from an uphill lie is a sand-shot challenge most pros and top amateurs find appetizing. Even average golfers who get queasy playing from the "beach" or the "bogey dust" know intuitively that an uphill bunker lie is far more playable than a downhill bunker lie. For tips on how to handle this challenge, we consult Jeff Howard, an instructor at Carolina National Golf Club in Bolivia, North Carolina.

Howard's first bit of advice is "Don't fight the slope as you take your stance." Translation: Don't dig in your spikes or manipulate your body to try to get the shoulders and hips dead level. Instead, allow them to tilt in accordance with the slope of the ground you're standing on. You'll have major problems getting the club head cleanly through impact if you "fight the slope."

In fact, adds Howard, "You might try to consciously feel your right shoulder staying down as you make your backswing." The shape of that backswing, he says, will be more V-shaped, or upright, and throughout it your hands must avoid swinging back behind you. What you want is a backswing that arcs "outside" the ball-to-target line.

Setup and backswing go a long way toward determining success on this shot. The rest of the drill is simple: Keep your lower body stable, open the club face slightly (a little less than you would on a level bunker lie), and swing about twice as hard as you would if playing a similar-length shot from rough instead sand.

"Don't be shy, give it a good blast," advises Howard, explaining that the uphill lie will naturally lift your golf ball vertically and cause it to carry a shorter distance. In addition, Howard says, the sand you're playing from is likely to be on the softer, more powdery side, "otherwise the ball would be unlikely to settle in that upslope position." Playing from soft-textured sand, he points out, you've got one more reason to swing with slightly extra force with no fear that the ball will explode out too far and too fast.

With a Fried-Egg Lie, Let the "Digger" Dig

Breakfast is long over, but there you are staring at a fried egg—a fried-egg lie in the bunker, that is. Not to worry, you've got the tool for the job: a sand wedge with a thick sole or flange and a pronounced "bounce angle"—i.e., a pronounced angle downward from the leading edge to the trailing edge—visible when you hold the club head at eye level with the shaft of the club perpendicular to the ground.

Charley Estes, head pro at New Sandy Burr Golf Course in Wayland, Massachusetts, gives the step-by-step for a bunker escape when your ball is half buried in the fried-egg style:

1. Grip your wedge with the leading edge square to the ball-target line, not open.
2. Place the ball in the middle of your stance. Stand fairly close and feel "tall to the ball," not hunched over. This posture will encourage a steep, V-shaped swing path.
3. Hit down sharply into the sand, about two inches behind the ball. Make an aggressive move and let yourself flow out of impact, finishing that chopping motion but not coming to a full follow-through.

"Your wedge is designed to be a natural digger," says Estes, "and all you're really doing with this setup and swing is letting the digger dig." The ball will react to this digger swing by popping out on a particularly vertical angle, then floating toward your target and landing with forward "release," rather than backspin "bite." Once on the green, you can accept compliments and rest assured that percentages suggest you'll have many more normal bunker lies before you encounter your next fried egg.

Swing Easy and Pick It Clean from Fairway Bunkers

You aren't just in a sand bunker, you're also lying 140 yards from the green: While that may sound like double trouble to most average golfers, teaching professional Ronnie Johnson points out some positives.

▶ Your lie is usually level.

▶ The bunker lip you have to get over is usually waist-high or lower.

▶ You can often get away with a "mistake"—the skulled or bladed shot—that would be disastrous from greenside bunkers.

"Playing from a fairway bunker, you are definitely programming, if not a skull, then a thin hit," says Johnson, who recently worked with his brother, Rocquee Johnson, in preparation for Rocquee's appearance in the U.S. Senior Open. "To do that, you position the ball forward in your stance and be sure to make an easy backswing and smooth motion into the ball." Other setup fundamentals are similar to a fairway shot, according to Johnson: no need to choke down on the club and, in his opinion, no particular need to keep the lower body still, which we sometimes hear in fairway-bunker how-to articles.

As for club selection, Johnson advises taking one extra club, two extra clubs if the lie is bumpy. He says, "Without a smooth lie, you won't be able to pick it as cleanly, and the extra sand you take will kill some of your trajectory" and, therefore, your distance.

Chapter 9

Specialty Bunker Shots

Use More Club for Longer Explosion Shots

There's no law that says we can only step into a bunker located up by the green if we're holding a standard, heavy-soled sand wedge. When the explosion shot you face is from a bunker that's separated from the green by 10 or 15 yards, Don Allan, of Hillandale Golf Course in Durham, North Carolina, would like to see you head in there with a pitching wedge, a nine-iron, or even an eight-iron.

"Golfers would find it easier to use a pitching wedge or nine-iron from bunkers near the green if they realized they were simply hitting a ball out of sand, not digging it out of a tar pit," laughs Allan.

Here are his simple instructions for the long greenside explosion:

▶ When you take a less-lofted iron into a bunker, you can generally cut down the length of your swing a bit, which will give you more control.

▶ Think of the long explosion in simple terms: You supply the power, but the club does the actual work. As long as you don't decelerate coming into impact, a controlled but decisive swing will supply plenty of that escape power.

▶ Place the ball in the center of your stance and keep the legs quiet. No need to drive them forward. Also, your stance at address should be square to the target line, not opened up.

▶ In accord with your stance, the leading edge of the iron should be square at address, not turned open.

▶ With this combination of a stronger-lofted club and a "toned down" swing, you'll also want to take a little less sand than you would with a heavy sand wedge. Therefore, make a less steeply angled swing than you normally would in a green-area bunker.

▶ Execute your decisive, non decelerating swing, and look for the ball to come out slightly lower than on most bunker shots, though still plenty high to clear a normal lip. When it lands, it will have enough spin to settle down after completing its initial hop, skip and roll.

And if the lip of the bunker is too high or you haven't practiced this shot the way you told yourself you would, "just switch to a regular sand wedge," advises Cramer, "and hit a basic escape shot. It may not reach the green, but at least you won't be playing two shots in a row from the same bunker."

Coming Out of the Cacti:
Recovery from Desert

Environmental laws prevent course builders from turning a Southwest desert landscape into wall-to-wall turfgrass. The result is photogenic contrast between the green fairways of a desert golf course and the harsh badlands to either side. Tyler Pingel, a professional at Troon North Club in Scottsdale, Arizona, knows the recovery shot from desert scrub and sand all too well. Here's what he tells his students.

Avoid danger and use common sense. "Most courses clean out the underbrush along fairways," says Pingel, "but you still could find yourself among the yucca plant and the Spanish dagger. If you hit it into the scrub and can't see your ball fairly soon, play what we call the 'desert rule' and take a drop laterally on the fairway, with a penalty of one stroke. They don't want you spending too much time in the desert areas, due to snakes." If your ball is in the clear and you've got room to swing, here's the technique to use:

1. Put the ball back in your stance and lean your weight slightly to the front foot. "You've usually got a fairly firm lie and you're trying to pick the ball clean," says Pingel.

2. Pinch the ball with a descending blow. "What you have is a crusty surface that your club head will break up as it strikes the ball," Pingel explains. "Under that is usually powdery sand, which you don't want to get involved with." So think of your club head as cracking the crust as it propels the ball, then continuing forward without going any deeper into the soft undersurface.

When Down in the Southeast, Escape Easily from "Waste" Areas

New or remodeled golf courses in Florida and throughout the Southeast tend to feature long, flat, ungrassed stretches beside fairways that are known as "waste areas." Local professionals like Samm Wolfe, of the Palmetto Dunes Resort in Hilton Head, South Carolina, consider these areas "more of a bonus than a trap."

By "bonus," Wolfe simply means that the surface is usually clear (except for decorative plantings in a few spots) and simple to play off. He compares it much more closely to old-fashioned Texas hardpan than to the scrub/sand/snakebite areas found alongside fairways in the desert Southwest.

"The waste area's surface," says Wolfe, "is crushed, compacted shells—very firm and consistent, and fairly forgiving of a shot that doesn't cleanly strike the ball. People on vacation psych themselves out on waste-area shots because they think they're hitting from soft sand."

To play an iron shot from this type of lie, take one extra club than normal from that distance and position the ball back in your stance, advises Wolfe. Choke down slightly on your grip; make a V-shaped, three-quarters swing, and aim to a fairly safe part of the fairway or green. "You haven't put yourself in jail by landing in a waste area," says Wolfe, "but you're still not in Position A for attacking the pin." Translation: Anything on the green or very close to it should make you happy.

The Shallow Bunker Shortcut Escape: Putt It Out

New golf courses feature "green complexes" with bulging mounds and scooped-out bunkers. Land in the sand at these layouts and you're certain to need your sand wedge.

But many older courses feature bunkers (especially toward the backs of their greens) that are shallow and fairly level, with barely a lip at all where the sand ends and the greenside collar begins. Next time you find yourself in one of these, you might think of "beating the system" by playing out with a putter. Jim Fitzgerald, pro at the Chevy Chase Club in Bethesda, Maryland, explains how.

"By selecting a putter," Fitzgerald explains, "you allow yourself to hit the ball itself." The downside is that you need a good 15 or 20 feet from the edge of the bunker to the pin to allow your firmly putted ball to slow down. If it feels like there is only enough room to tap the putt, your risk of not getting it out will be quite high.

For the bunker putt, position the ball toward your front foot and lean your weight forward. Now you can make a level putting stroke and not worry about hitting sand first. "Figure on a stroke that's about half again as forceful as it would be from that same distance on the green," advises Fitzgerald. "Crossing the sand and the grassy collar of the green will take a lot of the speed out of the shot."

And since you're beating the system, don't get too greedy and try to hole the shot. The point is to produce a sand recovery that you're certain will work out better than if you played a standard explosion shot with your wedge.

Wet or Stiff Sand: Whether to Explode Out or "Pick It"

It's rare these days that a golfer encounters extremely soft, powdery sand that grabs hold of his most thick-soled wedge and creates a puff effect that keeps the ball from leaving the hazard. More often, courses err on the side of stiff, grainy sand, which is a challenge on its own but "gets downright intimidating," according to instructor Kris Kallem, under wet conditions. Here are Kallem's guidelines for playing from moist, packed sand in a greenside bunker.

▶ Decide whether to slide your wedge under it or actually try to hit "ball first" and "pick it out." You're not allowed to contact the surface with a practice swing, so the decision must be made by visually inspecting the sand and feeling it with your feet. (With any luck, one of your buddies will encounter the first bunker shot on a day when sand is that firm and stiff.)

▶ If you decide to explode the ball (i.e., hit sand only and have the sand you dig up propel the ball), Kallem, of Fairways Golf Course in Cheney, Washington, suggests you play it back a bit in your stance, open the club face, and swing forcefully but not steeply down on the ball. "Even though you've positioned the ball back in your stance," says Kallem, "you need to come in at a moderate angle if you want to keep the wedge moving through impact." Even a successful explosion from these conditions won't carry the ball as far as the swing feels like it should, so be sure not to throttle back.

▶ If you decide to pick the ball out, select a wedge that works well from the fairway (one without much bounce angle to its flange), open your body and feet to the target line, and swing sharply at the bottom of the back of the ball. "Feel a little dead-wristed on this shot," says Kallem. "The ball will likely come out with some left-to-right sidespin on it, so look for it to roll to the right after it lands."

In the Bunker and Up by the Lip?
Swing Upslope and Hope

When your ball somehow comes to rest up by the lip of a greenside bunker, the first fundamental, according to Nick Saymanski, of South Toledo Golf Club in Toledo, Ohio, is to tell yourself clearly that you are "dealing with a bad break, and anything out is good."

With that pressure-relieving thought in mind, proceed as follows:

▶ Select a sand wedge that has plenty of loft and lots of "bounce." (Bounce, once again, is a measurement of the angle from the leading edge to the trailing edge of a wedge's sole).

▶ Take your stance with both feet deeply planted, but with your stance open to the target line and shoulders and hips conforming to the upslope of the bunker wall. Open the blade of the wedge at address and grip firmly.

▶ Swinging with the upslope, enter the sand early—several inches behind the ball. Keep the club head moving through the sand and out.

If there's no room on the other side of the ball to actually get the club head out and moving toward follow-through, you'll have to leave the club head buried and just "hiccup" the ball forward, as Saymanski colorfully puts it. If at all possible, however, you should endeavor to extract both club head and ball from the sand. Either way, the ball won't travel far, but since it won't have backspin it should roll at least several feet toward the cup.

Playing from the Bunker with One Foot Out

This is a problem that comes along rarely, but Stephanie Malone, of Broadmoor Golf Club in Seattle, wants to arm you with a solution all the same. We're talking about the sand shot in which the ball is resting so close to the bunker's edge that the player must stand at address with one foot outside the hazard. Here's what to do:

"As you take your stance," says Malone, "make sure to lean with the slope of the terrain. The leg that is outside the bunker may have to be bent at the knee with the foot rolled inward or only the toe braced against the ground." Needless to say, you'll need to fuss around a bit to make sure you achieve good balance at address.

"Grip down on the club, to get closer to the ball," Malone advises. "Lay the club face somewhat open and take a fairly full swing. Since you'll be swinging down into the sand, the ball won't run very much when it lands, so don't hold back with the swing." Because of your compromised stance, it will be "tough to release through impact," says Malone, so be doubly sure not to quit on the shot. "And remember the situation," she counsels. "You've gotten a bad break, and if you can do anything at all successful with this recovery shot, give yourself an extra pat on the back."

Chapter 10

Short Game:
Attack Shots

Tips on Holing the "Birdie Chip"

The pros call it a "birdie chip," and teaching pro Jacques Panet-Raymond says half the battle for amateur golfers is simply knowing this opportunity when they see it.

"You've missed the green with your approach shot," says Panet-Raymond, setting the scene, "but you're only a few paces off the putting surface, in light rough, and your whole shot measures just 15 to 25 feet." Often in cases like this, there are one or more players on the green itself who have more ground to cover than you have, and less chance of making birdie.

"Play this shot with a lower lofted iron, not a sand wedge or even a pitching wedge," advises Panet-Raymond. "It will only be in the air a short part of the way—you're trying to turn your chip shot into a putt as soon as possible." That's a key point, to get the ball settled and rolling like a putt by at least halfway to the cup, if not sooner. "Make sure to play from a good lie and don't break your wrists as you bring the hands through impact. Make a putting-style stroke, not a wristy stroke."

Because of the club you've chosen and the firm-wristed stroke you make, the ball won't have backspin on it, and it will run its natural course much as a putt would—hopefully ending up in the cup or close enough for a tap-in.

To Make More Birdies, Learn the Pitch Shot with Bite

Your ball is in fairway or light rough, about 30 yards away from the hole, and you're playing a shot that you would like to see land in the neighborhood of the flag, skip once or twice, then bite and hold. For the average player, this is as close as we get to the show-off shot in which our ball lands with backspin "juice" and actually sucks back toward the point it was played from. In reality, say the teaching pros, it's just as valuable as that moonwalker shot you see on TV.

Mike Bender, professional at Timicuan Golf and Country Club in Lake Mary, Florida, is the pro with today's recipe for an aggressive pitch shot from a good lie, with "bite."

▶ Using a sand wedge (one with a relatively thin sole), play the ball back in your stance, off the right foot.

▶ Feel your hands "ahead," or closer to the target than the ball is, at address.

▶ Don't fiddle with your grip. "The club face will appear to be hooded or closed," says Bender. "That's due to it being back in your stance. You'll get used to that look, just keep the face aimed straight at the hole."

▶ Take the club back naturally, allowing hands and club head to work inside the ball-to-target line.

▶ On the downswing, make more of a descending blow than you would on most iron shots. "You should feel crisp impact, and you'll probably nip off a small divot," says Bender.

A good general thought: "Don't let the club pass the hands," Bender intones. The initial result of all this will be a slightly lower ball flight than you normally get with a sand wedge, then touchdown up toward the pin and a biting finish that should leave its share of makeable birdie bids.

Approach Cautiously, Then Putt Boldly on Classic Below-the-Hole Courses

Particularly in the northern tier of the United States, where cool-weather bentgrass can be cut way down to make a glassy putting surface, there are many ball-below-the-hole golf courses, with greens sloping back to front, that penalize a player for hitting approach shots to the back of the green. From that precarious position, the next stop can be somewhere back on the fairway, putting or chipping back uphill.

John Nowobilski, one of Connecticut's top players from the club-pro ranks, routinely advises his members at Tolland Country Club in Hebron on scoring strategies at this type of golf course. Nowobilski's advice includes the following nuggets:

▶ Be extra careful getting your yardage for approach shots on this type of hole, particularly when the pin is cut toward the front.

▶ Subtract at least five yards from the yardage to the pin and aim to settle your ball on that spot.

▶ When the pin is cut middle or back, don't be too disappointed with an approach that stops toward the front of the green—it may be a more advantageous position than if you were hole-high and facing a side-breaking putt.

▶ When playing greenside recovery shots, especially from lies that are above the hole, be ready to pick a landing spot that is fairly far from the hole. With luck, you'll be able to use a swale or hollow in the green to take the speed off your chip or pitch and settle in a safe, below-the-hole position.

▶ Use extra "imagery and feel" in your pitching, chipping, and putting on these greens. Watch other players' shots carefully and learn from what you see.

Nowobilski points out an ironic truth about this type of green: Although there are many approach and recovery shots that have to be played tenderly rather than boldly, the putt that is set up by a properly cautious approach can be a firm, aggressive uphill run at the hole.

When the Hole Is on a Top Tier, Play the "Dead Cat" Pitch

Professional instructors distinguish between chipping and pitching simply: The chip is a short approach that has minimum air time, maximum ground time, while the pitch is vice versa—maximum air time, minimum ground time. Between the two, they favor the chip as a higher-percentage shot, simply because getting your ball out of the air and rolling on the green requires less finesse and control than lofting it a prescribed distance and getting it to stop quickly.

But when a pin is placed on the top tier of a green, or you

have a hazard partially in the way of your direct line to the cup, maximum air time is called for, and the ball has to settle almost immediately upon arrival. This is sometimes called the "dead cat" pitch, and Kevin Greubner, of Sycamore Hills Golf Club in Mount Clemens, Michigan, has sound advice on how to play it.

"First of all, you need a clean lie to play from," says Greubner. "You'll be trying to carry the ball about three-quarters of the distance to your target." Start by opening up the club face of your most lofted wedge and leaning your weight slightly forward, Greubner advises. "The feel of this stroke will be a little wristy," he says, "so don't set up with your hands ahead and the shaft of your wedge tilted toward the hole, as you would with pitch-and-run shot. Let the shaft rest fairly vertical to the ground at address."

As for the swing itself, "it's got a roundish shape, but not the U shape some people expect," Greubner notes. "And you've got to swing your wedge, not guide it, through impact. Feel like you are nipping the ball off the turf, and taking a little divot that starts right at the back of the ball. Don't hit behind the ball." To limit the force and distance of the shot, limit your backswing—make sure not to swing back too far, then decelerate through impact. "The 'dead cat' pitch goes up fairly high, but not as high as some people think. It's got backspin on it, so it doesn't need to come in vertically to settle quickly."

Chapter 11

Short Game: Safety Shots

Swing Thoughts and Reminders for Razor-Sharp Chipping

We could all struggle as we play the more awkward greenside shots and still post decent scores if we would only master the basic chip-and-run stroke from fair lies within 25 yards of the hole. Jim Fitzgerald, head pro at the Chevy Chase Club in Bethesda, Maryland, has collected or invented a whole portfolio of chipping tips and concepts, a selection of which is presented here:

▶ Get the feel by grabbing steel: Your friends will arrive at the course in ten minutes and you're hitting practice chips while you wait. Before you start, take your wedge and grip it about midway down, well onto the steel. Make your basic chipping motion—shoulders hinging, wrists staying firm, in midair. The club handle should stay well clear of your left side. If it hits or comes near your ribs, you're breaking your wrists, a chipping no-no.

▶ Strike the side of your bag: Lay your golf bag down beside the green and lightly strike it with your wedge using the chip stroke. The back of your left wrist should be straight and your right wrist will be bent. Feel the firmness in your left wrist that prevents any flipping motion your right hand might instinctively try to trigger.

▶ Sweep grass: Place a ball in light rough outside the collar of the green. Take your wedge and step back from the ball one pace. Set up in the classic chipping position—feet slightly open, a choked-down grip on the club, hands ahead of the club face. Now sweep the tips of the grass using a putting-style stroke from the shoulders. The sole of your wedge should brush the grass for a span of six or eight inches, not digging into the turf at any point. Do ten of these sweep strokes, then step up and chip the ball without changing your motion at all.

Chipping, as Fitzgerald's concepts show, is as much about the things you don't do as it is about the things you do. These reminders are easily practiced anytime a wristy inconsistency enters your chipping stroke.

Choose Your Chipping Club by the Numbers

Most good chippers, according to Dave Collins of Boise, Idaho, change the club they chip with based on the distance to be covered, the slope of the green, and the type of rough or fairway they are playing from. Collins, a widely published and sought-after instructor who operates a golf academy at Shadow Valley Golf Course, has developed a brilliant little formula for club selection in the chipping game.

"If you can putt, you can chip," says Collins, by way of introducing his formula. "The key to being a good chipper is having the right club in your hand. Use this formula, and I can promise you will get up and down nine times out of ten." Collins doesn't say it, but that tenth time, by his prediction, should be a hole-out. Here's how the formula works:

Wherever you are chipping from—three paces off the green, five paces, whatever—locate a spot *one pace onto* the green. Designate that as your *landing spot*. From here there are two more variables: (1) how many paces from your ball to that landing spot? and (2) how many paces from that spot to the hole? Divide ball position–to–landing spot into landing spot–to–hole, and you'll come up with a ratio that is 1:1, 1:2, and so on, up to 1:6. For example, when it's three paces from your ball to the landing spot and 9 paces from that spot to the hole, you're dividing three into 9 to get the 1:3 ratio. As the club selection chart below shows, a 1:3 ratio calls for the eight-iron. Here are the rest of the correspondences:

Club	Carry/Roll Ratio
PW	1:1
nine-iron	1:2
eight-iron	1:3
seven-iron	1:4
six-iron	1:5
five-iron	1:6

Learn this club selection system and follow it, Collins promises, and you will save stroke upon stroke around the green. Make slight adjustments for significant upslopes and downslopes. (Note: You do not have to actually land your ball on the designated spot as long as you make a decent chip. Land short of it and you'll get extra run; land past it and you'll get less run.)

When Just Off the Green, Do You Chip or Putt?

Faced with the question of whether to putt or chip from off the green, some amateurs putt virtually every time. These are golfers with little or no confidence in their chipping ability. What they don't realize, suggests Brian Natzel, of the professional staff at Garland Resort in Gaylord, Michigan, is how similar the short chipping stroke is to their putter stroke. Understanding that short-game fundamental, they could make their decision about how to play little shots through the collar and fairway edge a lot more productively.

There's one basic question to answer, according to Natzel, namely, can you make a smooth putting stroke from the position you're in? Or is there so much fuzz, "frog hair," and distance (including upslope) to get through before reaching the hole that you'll be swinging the putter too hard to control it?

In that case, Natzel advises using a lofted iron, such as the pitching wedge, nine-iron, or eight-iron. "Three feet of collar might be just right for putting," he says. "Six or eight feet of fairway and collar combined is probably too much." The other advantage to using an iron instead of the "Texas wedge" is that irons come in varieties, allowing you to make basically the same-length stroke—adjusting for distance and slope via club selection—every time you encounter these situations. That will improve your consistency and save strokes.

But again, to get past the deceptive "security blanket" factor of always wanting to putt from off the green, merely understand that the chipping stroke you need here is almost identical to the simple no-wrist, back-and-through stroke you make with your trusty putter.

"Chip" with a Metal Wood When There's Lots of Shaved Grass to Cover

These days, golf course grooming provides more and more closely mown playing surface in the vicinity of the green. Sure there's rough and bunkers to contend with, but you're increasingly likely to be off the green with very tightly mown mounds and swales between you and the actual green. In these instances, a wedge is tricky to use because the location of those first few bounces is hard to predict—some landing spots would speed the shot up decisively, some would slow it down.

As an alternative, you could putt the ball, but a putter head and shaft aren't designed to propel a golf ball a long distance over grass that, though shaved, is still considerably higher than green height and tall enough to create the friction that robs a putted ball of speed.

The club you simply have to try in this situation is your metal three-wood or even your metal driver. Dave Bobber, of Trappers Turn Golf Club in Wisconsin Dells, Wisconsin, sees the following benefits to the "metal wood chip":

▶ Impact is crisp and lively off the face, even though you haven't moved the club with much force.

▶ The solid spot on the club face is much harder to miss with a metal wood than with a putter.

▶ The loft angle on a metal three-wood is enough to give the ball an initial "skim" effect along the grass, but not enough to get it hopping in an uncontrolled manner.

How to play this shot? "Choke down considerably on the grip," says Bobber, "while still standing comfortably. Make a putting- or chipping-style stroke (i.e., not wristy), just focusing on solid contact." Your path into the ball will be shallow, not steep, "unless your ball is just in the rough, with the short grass a foot or so away," says Bobber. "In that case you'll have to hit down on it somewhat."

Bobber's final comment on this increasingly popular shot is his most relevant one. "You absolutely have to practice this shot before you try it on the golf course," he intones. "But most golfers," he adds, "won't have to practice it for very long before they start to get the hang of it."

The Greenside Lob Looks Harder Than It Is

You've missed another green and your ball is in medium rough with a bunker between you and your chosen landing spot. The only choice is to take your most lofted wedge and float the ball over that bunker. If this little challenge tends to confound you (translation: you end up dumping the ball in the bunker five times out of ten), take the advice of Randy Tupper, pro at Clear Creek Golf Club in Vicksburg, Mississippi. Most of what Tupper advises involves technique, but he also addresses the psychological facet.

The proper mindset, according to Tupper, is to think of this shot as being more full-out and aggressive than you tend to think. The swing motion it requires is closer to a full fairway wedge from 110 yards than a tender little downhill chip from above the hole—especially if your lie is below the green, which it often is when playing over a sand trap. Here's the step-by-step instruction:

1. Set up with an open stance, the ball a little forward, and the blade of the wedge slightly open.

2. At address, make sure your hands are ahead of the club head ("Optically, it can appear your hands are ahead when they're actually on-line with the blade," warns Tupper. "Make sure you account for that illusion and really get the hands ahead.")

3. Focus on keeping those hands ahead throughout impact and follow-through. "The pros hit this shot with a flat left wrist. The amateur comes into impact with the left wrist bent, like they're trying to flip the club head and help the ball get airborne," Tupper says. "The ball will rise up on a steep trajectory because of the loft angle of your wedge, not some angle of your wrist."

4. Keep a little extra weight on your front foot—this will automatically cause your swing to go back and come down steeply, which is what you want.

5. Make a fairly full backswing and hit down on the ball. "Feel yourself pressing the ball into the ground," he says. "It won't happen, but that's what you should feel." And never, ever let the club head decelerate.

The amount of force you're imparting on this shot may give you the feeling you're carrying the shot twice as far as you should. That, too, is an illusion, because the high amount of backspin a properly struck lob shot imparts will reduce the carry distance markedly. Backspin will also cause the ball to settle quickly on the green.

Collar Escapes: The Bellied Wedge and the Hammerhead Putter

Dense, three-inch rough encircling greens is a give-and-take proposition. It forms a grass wall to hold your golf ball on the putting surface, but it's difficult to recover from when your ball is cozied right up tight to it. Nick Saymanski, a pro at South Toledo Golf Club in Toledo, Ohio, offers two makeshift but tour-proven ways to play a ball that is sitting on the green but resting against a thick stand of greenside rough.

"The first option, for me, is to turn my putter counter-clockwise 90 degrees so the face points toward my feet and the blunt end of the toe is lined up to strike the ball," says Saymanski. With his putter in this "hammerhead" orientation, Saymanski plays the ball slightly forward in his stance, makes a normal putting stroke, contacts the ball with the blunt, toe end of his putter head, and follows through naturally. The putter is coming through the grass the long way and thus encounters little or no resistance. "Focus on making solid contact on the center of the ball," advises Saymanski. "You don't have to force the stroke." Struck squarely, the ball will "come out rolling, not jump or bounce," he says.

For players whose putters are too narrow or aren't squared off at the tip, the other option from this spot is the "bellied" wedge. Take your most thick-soled wedge and, using the setup and stroke described above, strike the ball with the sole of the club, "the part that says 'SW' on it," says Saymanski. The sole of the wedge, built to ride through sand, will also ride through your patch of rough—as long as you're content to use that sole surface to strike the ball. Again, don't force the stroke, just play it as a putt, focus on centered contact, and let the ball roll toward the hole.

Chapter 12

Getting Out of Jail

Iron Escapes from Thick and Wiry Rough

Come U.S. Open time, golf fans get to see big-name pros making some swings from heavy rough that start out fiercely and end up looking awkward. And those are golf's strongest players. Escaping with a middle to short iron from rough that's high and wiry is not the time to try winning a beauty contest with your swing, according to Kris Kallem, who teaches at Fairways Golf Course in Cheney, Washington.

"You have to forget some of the rules of a model golf swing in these conditions," says Kallem. "For starters—and this is the only time you'll hear me say this—you have to grip the club very tightly on this shot. On a grip-pressure scale from one to ten, grip it at about an eight or nine," he counsels. And aim as far right as you feel you safely can, because the tendency of this type of grass is to grab your club by the hosel, which swings the club face shut and sends the ball mysteriously far left of your line.

"You also have to swing very hard," says Kallem, "which is another swing trait teachers usually discourage but which happens to apply here." Play the ball in the middle of your stance or a bit forward, and select a club with plenty of loft. That may have to be a wedge, if the lie looks so gnarly that no stronger-lofted club will actually get to the ball and create solid impact. In lies that are slightly less devilish, feel free to play a seven- or eight-iron, says Kallem, "but don't expect it go more than about 70 percent of its normal distance."

Planning and Executing Your Escape from Trees

They've got no shortage of trees in Portland, Oregon, which makes Ryan Davis, of Portland's Columbia Edgewater Country Club, a good source for tips on how to escape from them. For starters, consider taking an unplayable lie if you're deep into the treeline and liable to ricochet your next shot unpredictably. If you're only a few yards deep and various escape routes present themselves, Davis advises high-percentage routes over high-risk ones.

"Eight times out of ten you can only play back to the fairway, not play for the green," says Davis. Once you've accepted that, check out the yardage remaining. If a totally risk-free chip is going to leave you 200 yards out, and a route that is just a little bit chancy can get you comfortably to 160, that slight risk may be worth taking. The lie will help tell you whether a fairly ambitious shot can be played. Too much brush, leaves, or straw in the way and your plans to really advance the ball should be shelved.

The standard advancement shot from in the trees will need to come out low. Here's how Davis sets up and plays this recovery. "Take a three-iron or four-iron and choke down an inch or two," he advises. "If you have to hook the ball, set the club behind the ball with the club face pointing directly at your initial target line, then stand at address with your shoulders, hips, and feet pointed considerably right of that line. Take the club back about half the normal amount and swing in control, without decelerating—don't get quick, even though it's a partial swing. You should feel a nice punch at impact."

Most importantly, you should swing along the line established by your feet at address. You'll be creating a hooking sidespin, without any manipulation of your hands to try to "help the hook." The variance between your club face angle and the line of your feet, hips, and shoulders will, Davis promises, put the desired hook spin on the ball and get it to "turn the corner" toward the green.

For a similar shot from the opposite treeline—which would require a slicing sidespin—use the same technique, only align your body to the left of the initial line of flight you want the ball to travel on. "Remember, it's a smooth, partial swing that creates a punch feeling at impact," summarizes Davis. "That comes from shortening up the backswing and follow-through—let it happen on its own."

Hit a Rainbow Over That One Pesky Tree

When a skier has occasion to curse the placement of a certain tree, it's likely he has a splint or a cast in his future. When a golfer has one single tree bedeviling him, the only professional help needed is from someone like Brian Bryson, who teaches at Hartefeld National in Avondale, Pennsylvania. In Bryson's arsenal of escape shots, the big rainbow shot over a mature tree is listed as a true hero shot that is rewarding to pull off and often fun just to try.

That said, he begins his minilesson on this shot by requiring students to evaluate whether discretion isn't more called for—in the form of a sideways wedge to some unobstructed area of the fairway. In making that decision, look at the shot you wish to play from the side. Assuming you can lift your ball about 10 to 20 percent higher than normal via certain stance and swing adjustments, will it get high enough soon enough to clear the top branches? Secondarily, will the trajectory that gets it over the tree give the ball a chance to land on the green? "Having it land a little short isn't so bad," says Bryson, "but if you're likely to end up with a 50-yard pitch shot even if you clear the tree, it isn't worth the risk."

How to play the shot: "Start by opening your stance a few inches and opening the club face slightly," says Bryson. "Play the ball slightly forward in your stance." (Note: An uphill lie will certainly help you succeed with this shot, but if you've got a downhill lie or a decidedly sidehill lie, Bryson suggests you don't even attempt it.) Your swing should be extra-vertical, with a slightly shortened backswing.

"Concentrate on hitting down on the ball with an aggressive swing in which 'all the hinges' (shoulders, wrists, club shaft) are used to the fullest," advises Bryson. "Allow the loft of the club to do the work." Although you are making a big swing, he points out, you may not finish with your weight fully shifted or your shoulders turned so that the club is wrapped behind you, due to the vertical nature of the club path. This is a shot where visualization is particularly important, according to

Bryson. "Picture your ball rising up and clearing the tree," he says. "It's a fun shot, so let it fly and don't hold back."

Play from the Water as You Would from Sand

All but one or two balls in 100 that enter a water hazard result in a penalty stroke and the need for a drop. But once in a while, shallow water at the edge of the pond or creek will leave the ball at least partly above the water line and offering its owner the chance for a heroic escape with no penalty.

Sean Sundra, of Stonebridge Golf Club in Monroe, North Carolina, explains when a water escape is possible and how to pull it off.

"First off, you have to evaluate the lie," says Sundra. "Look for less than two-thirds of the ball to be immersed and for the ball to be at rest, not moving." (Rule 14-6 does allow you to play a ball that's moving in a water hazard, but it's not a recommended strategy for most amateurs.)

The club Sundra recommends is the sand wedge you use from bunkers—the one with the biggest "bounce" angle. As you stand over the shot, remember an important bit of physics: "Water is actually denser than sand," Sundra notes, "so by nature it's going to offer even more resistance to the club head as it tries to enter."

The golfer adjusts to this reality by choosing an entry spot in the water that's a good four to six inches behind the ball. Any closer and you'll skull the ball, pushing it down instead of lifting it out.

"You never actually contact the ball with your club head," says Sundra. "What you're doing is displacing water, and the water carries the ball out of the hazard. People are surprised, but water actually propels a golf ball more efficiently than sand, so you can get some good carry if you make the right swing." Make a steep backswing, commit to the shot, don't quit at impact, and finish with your belt buckle toward the target. Escape cleanly and you won't even mind the mud spatters.

Up Against the Wrong Side of a Tree?
Flip Over a Seven-Iron

Golf has a piece of time-honored escape artistry that most average players consider a show-off shot but is considered by teaching pros to be easier than it looks. We're talking about the upside-down lofted iron that turns a righty golfer into a temporary lefty (or vice versa) and allows him to lay a meaty, well-weighted end of his iron onto the golf ball and extract it from the base of whatever tree or post is keeping him from swinging from the conventional side.

The step-by-step on this shot, per Dave Johnson, of Rancho Canada Golf Course in Carmel, California, is as follows:

1. Check to see if a root is blocking your club's path enough to cause a whiff. If so, proceed under Rule 28, Ball Unplayable, and take relief under penalty of one stroke within two club lengths.
2. If no roots interfere, turn your club so the toe is pointed toward *your own* toes and grip with left-hand low or right-hand low (the equivalent of a cross-handed putting grip), whichever feels more natural.
3. Set up with a stable stance and keep your lower body still during backswing and downswing.

4. Make a short, simple, chipping-style swing, with your emphasis on making contact.

5. Be satisfied with any advancement of the ball toward a safe, playable lie. "Ten or 20 yards should be very satisfactory," says Johnson, especially if it gives you an angle to the hole that is significantly better than the angle from your drop area under the Ball Unplayable rule.

Chapter 13

Outthink the Architects

Choose Your Tees off the Par-3s

It might be a universal trick played by every greens crew member who sets up the tee markers before the day's play. On all 17 holes except Number 1, he paces off 20 to 25 yards between the blue tees and the whites—turning the seven-iron approach shot you would hit after driving from the whites into a demanding five-iron shot. On the 1st tee, however, that same crew man plants the blue markers only four to seven yards behind the whites. Without much time to think, and with your buddies and assorted onlookers wondering what kind of golfer you consider yourself, you calmly select the blue markers—and pay the price for that decision all day.

Matt Abramavicius, of Marengo Ridge Golf Club in Marengo, Illinois, advises the golfer who is playing a course for the first time to spend a minute looking at the scorecard and then choose his tee markers according to the yardage on the par-3s.

"If your handicap is 15 or above, which is most golfers," says Abramavicius, "you'll want to be hitting iron shots to the par-3s that are in the 140- to 175-yard range. Whichever set of tees gives you that yardage for the par-3 holes will also give you an appropriate course setup for your game on the par-4s and par-5s."

You Can "Fail Positively" When You Tee Up (and Aim) Wisely

This is a commonsense type of golf tip, but it takes on much greater meaning when explained by an actual course designer and expressed with the heavy emphasis and enthusiasm Brian Silva gives it.

Silva, of the architectural firm Cornish, Silva, and Mungeam, is the 1998 Architect of the Year as selected by *Golf World* magazine. He's also a critic of the setup work at many of today's courses, as in pins inappropriately located, tee markers in strange places, mowing patterns incorrect for the hole design, and so on.

But if he can say one thing about how a course is set up and how the average golfer should play it, Silva says this: Never aim for the middle of a fairway (or the middle of a green on a par-3) and never tee up in the middle of the tee markers.

Unless, that is, you are a straight-shot golfer whose typical ball flight doesn't drift or curve in one particular direction. That's the rare exception, of course; the rule is the player who—though 65 to 80 percent of his shots fade, slice, or get pushed right—tees up in the middle of the markers and aims for the middle of the fairway. By doing so, he basically cuts in half the fairway area he can legitimately play to.

"The average golfer can save six strokes a round—no exaggeration—by teeing up to one side of the teeing area and aiming down one side of the fairway," Silva declares. If he is prone to fading or slicing, he should tee up far right and aim down the left side of the fairway, the logic goes. "Doing that changes your focal point 15 or 20 yards," says Silva, "and it effectively widens your landing area by that much or more." If the ball stays straight, you're in the left rough and you've "failed positively," to use Silva's term. If it curves as expected, you end up on fairway instead of rough, or instead of in a hazard. "If you can predict your ball flight (on the shots that don't go dead straight) with average reliability," he concludes, "you can literally double the width of the fairway landing area you've been playing to. That's going to help your score more than any mechanical adjustment, and it's childishly simple to do."

Safe Driving on "Risk-Reward" Holes

In the golf vacation–land of the Southeast, where many courses are built around lakes and marshland, architects like to build L-shaped "risk-reward" driving holes. This sort of hole—usually a par-4 but sometimes a par-5—invites the golfer to "bite off" much of the hole's yardage with his drive, leaving himself a short iron shot onto the green.

It's exciting to step on the tee of these holes, noticing right away that your fairway swings (right or left) almost on an L, and no trees block you from trying to hit past the elbow of the hole. Golf professional Samm Wolfe, who hangs his shingle at the Hills Course of Palmetto Dunes Resort, shares some appropriate strategy for these goat-or-hero golf holes.

"To a player who likes taking risks and won't ruin his day by landing in the marsh," says Wolfe, "I would point out that these holes are characterized by particularly large landing areas off the tee." Even knowing that, Wolfe says, you ought to look carefully at your yardage guide. "Depth perception can really be thrown off by wide expanses," he notes. "And it only takes a couple of mounds fronting the fairway to make an airport runway look as small as a car hood." While this optical illusion may not bother you during practice swings, it could get you pushing the 'abort' light at the top of your backswing. Absorb all the data you can to make certain you stay committed until the swing is complete.

And don't have the decision made for you by someone else, suggests Wolfe. "Peer pressure is huge on these holes," he observes. One wise practice is to pull out your "comfort club," say a three-wood or four-wood, as soon as you step on the tee, setting your gaze directly onto the closest part of the fairway. "A marshland course that has one of these holes usually has two or three, so you could play safe once or twice and go for it the other time," says Wolfe.

It also matters whether the hole doglegs right or left. Wolfe has a grip pressure tip for the right-to-left golfer trying to bite off a big chunk of a risk-reward driving hole that swings left. "Squeeze the right hand a little bit," he offers. "That will keep you from turning the ball over too much and losing it to the left." In this type of situation, if your shot goes a little right of your intended line, the landing area gets bigger. As it curls left, you're looking at less and less solid ground and more hazard coming into play.

Play Better Golf Without Pins

Golf course architect Brian Silva has some inside information and a visual tip for average golfers that could make that next round lower-scoring and more enjoyable.

Silva's advice: Play the course with no pins in the greens.

"They say you need imagination to play golf well," Silva explains. "What I'm suggesting is that you use your imagination to remove the flagsticks from all 18 greens." His inside information, backing up the suggestion, is critical in nature and may be a bit disturbing to some.

"The pins you see on many public courses and even private clubs are cut in strange positions that the architect would never recommend, given the basic design of the hole, the placement of the tee markers and the conditions prevailing at that time of year," he says. "The cup-cutting job is usually given to an untrained junior member of the greens crew who probably got to work a half hour late that day and isn't giving much thought at all to where he is placing the holes. It's an important job, but I'm afraid it doesn't get a high priority at most courses."

Naturally, once you have played a par-4 or par-5 and have your ball up near the green but not on it, you can "put the pins back," mentally, and play your shot to the hole. But on all par-3s and on the longer shots to the par-4s and par-5s, see the green only as your target, not a flagstick. According to Silva, you'll be putting sooner and positioning yourself for more pars and fewer "big numbers."

Hit Accurate Shots Over the "Hidden Yardage"

Yes, the sprinkler heads and tee signs are marked with (usually) correct yardage from Point A to your target, but aren't there times you distrust what the markings say and hit less club than the distance suggests? We all do, and it's because course architects cleverly tempt us to by shaping the land in a manner that "hides" yardage and makes targets seem closer than they truly are.

Joe Villarreal, of Indian Summer Golf and Country Club in Olympia, Washington, doesn't begrudge the course designers their right to these optical illusions; he just wants to see his students outfox the architect, pick the proper club, and trust it.

"Public golfers play so many different courses, they end up in unfamiliar territory much more often than a club golfer," says Villarreal. "It's easy for them to get psyched out by a mound or a bunker that's only partway to the green site and hides the rest of that distance to the target."

Villarreal's solution is as follows:

▶ Take every map and yardage guide available out to a new course with you. Learn immediately which part of the green the marked yardages designate. Use the diagrams to spot course features that may obscure the actual lay of the land.

▶ On the first few holes of a new course (or even longer into the round) look backward from the landing areas and greens to the tees and to the spots you have played approaches from. On most holes, the little mysteries you see going in don't work in reverse. Ergo, you can see the distance you've covered plainly and understand how the course design might have been set up to fool you. This exercise will make you more resolute on the next shot where the posted yardage seems incorrect.

▶ Remember that the architect is paid to give solid, on-line drives and approaches ample landing area. If he doesn't, play will be held up and frustrated golfers will think twice about coming back. "Get an accurate yardage reading and go with it," says Villarreal. "Once you have your club selected, follow Harvey Penick's advice and 'take dead aim.'"

Nonhazardous Bunkers: The Ones You Actually Aim For

One of the headiest moments for any golfer comes when he first sets up over a three-wood shot to a par-5 with the full intention of knocking his ball into a greenside bunker. For most of us in the bogey-golf ranks, that's a counterintuitive play, but Bill MacLaughlin, of Crystal Lake Country Club in Pompano Beach, Florida, says it's part of the single-digit handicapper's playbook. Here are the criteria.

1. Bunker play can't be the weak link in your single-digit game. "You have to be honestly confident about getting up and down from the position you've put yourself in," says MacLaughlin.

2. It has to be the right type of trap. "Some bunkers are considered strategic," MacLaughlin explains. "They will grab shots hit by the weak player, but for the better player they only frame the shot and help him choose his line." Other bunkers, according to MacLaughlin, are considered "penal." These have high walls and difficult angles to that green's tougher pin positions. Architects

build these bunkers with the thought that sand saves will be a major challenge, even for top players. You play intentionally to strategic bunkers, not penal ones.

3. The alternative landing area has to be gnarly. "If you've got a good sand game, you're going to prefer a sandy lie to heavy rough on contoured ground," says MacLaughlin. "You'll get fewer awkward lies and more chance to spin the ball from sand," he points out. And, if there's lots of water around, the sand becomes a relatively safe harbor. "Sand and water are both hazards," MacLaughlin reminds us, "but there's no penalty stroke for going in the sand."

So yes, it would be a heady moment that first time you deliberately shoot to land in a bunker. But given golf's humbling nature, you might not make your intention known until you've hit the next shot onto the green.

Chapter 14

Course (and Score) Management

Learn to Play Wiser Around Water

Even though hitting out of bounds or losing a ball in the rough carries a more severe penalty, most average golfers experience their tensest moments when the hole they're playing is guarded by water. Garry Rippy, an instructor at Sugar Creek Country Club in Sugarland, Texas, tries to remove the "psych-out" factor from a water hole and get his students strategizing effectively around ponds, lakes, and creeks. Here are the highlights of what he tells them:

▶ On a par-4 or par-5 hole, isolate the shot that involves water and play that portion of the hole more conservatively. "On a shorter par-4 with water off the tee," says Rippy, "you can hit an iron or a five-wood knowing you'll land it safe and the water won't hound you anymore on that hole." With fears of a splash behind you, this thinking goes, you can return to bold strategizing.

▶ Think about where you would drop if your ball were to land in the water hazard. "If it's a creek that crosses in front of the green, that's just one stroke and you're still just hitting a little pitch," says Rippy. "With a large pond that comes right up to the front of the tee, you're basically playing your third from between the markers. Think one step ahead to decide how cautious you need to be."

▶ That includes taking careful note of any pond with a steep bank leading down to it. "Some ponds and lakes have such steep banks that half the people who go in take a drop, then hit their next ball in the water, as well," muses Rippy, referring to the chancy hanging lie of the dropped ball.

▶ The way modern courses shape the mounds and hollows adjacent to water hazards tends to increase the hazards' effective size. "A creek may be only eight feet wide in terms of actual water," he says, "but if the ground slopes down to it and the grass there is cut short, that creek may play at 15 or 20 feet wide."

▶ On par-3s that are all carry over water, take one or two extra clubs. "Start by getting the correct yardage," he urges, "then add 10 or more yards for the carry."

And if you do land in a water hazard, don't let the shame we all feel at making our ball splash linger. Add the one penalty stroke and think how you would feel if that stroke was caused by having to take an unplayable lie up against a tree or shrub. "The added stroke is your penalty," Rippy says. "Don't compound the penalty by getting down on yourself. If you do, it will usually carry over to your next shot."

Why You Should Take a Playing Lesson

Your typical day on the links divides into highlights and lowlights—the thrill of a side-door birdie putt that drops and the frustration of a "snowman" triple-bogey on some reachable par-5. If these emotional highs and lows define the golf experience for you, then the comments you'll hear prior to an on-course lesson with Chuck Wike may seem odd.

"Before we start a playing lesson," says Wike, an award-winning instructor who includes many tour pros among the students at his Classic Swing Golf Academy in Surfside Beach, South Carolina, "we put a ban on nouns and adjectives when the student is evaluating what he's done on a hole. We accept numbers only: 3, 4, 5, 8, 10, whatever. If you knock in a 40-footer for 3, that's not birdie, that's just one lower than 4, one higher than 2. Words get us excited or get us upset, and then the game gets harder to play."

The playing lesson—two hours or so on the course with a pro and a few other students—is one of golf's great untapped educational resources. According to Wike, the golf academy setting has made playing lessons more available. Thinking of taking one? Look around for a curriculum that stresses the nonmechanical concepts emphasized by Wike and his staff, including:

▶ How to "open the hole up" by choosing a certain route to the flag and avoiding another. "We get a student in the habit of playing toward one feature and playing away from another, depending on what gives them the best odds of success," says Wike.

▶ Managing the round by that day's ball flight. "No swing mechanics on the course during that playing lesson," intones Wike. "They learn to play their round with what they've got, then fix it later."

▶ Make yardage calculation and preshot planning second-nature. "It's not just the sprinkler head over there, it's how many paces from that sprinkler head to you," Wike lectures. "It's not just that yardage, it's the yardage to center, front, and the flag. Then you factor wind, then elevation, then carry, then your lie, then choose a club. Our playing-lesson students get blown away by the preshot detail," says Wike, who demands that students make these calculations at tour-pro pace so that play isn't slowed and the student's own rhythm isn't fouled up.

▶ Learn your swing and recognize your psych-out shots. We all have shots that don't just challenge us, they psych us out. In a playing lesson, make sure to point out these intimidators to the teaching pro. He or she will explain what it is about your setup and swing that makes these shots particularly tough for you, and how to take the fear factor out so you can at least have a go at the shot.

P.S. When your game and your 18-hole scores do improve, you are fully entitled to haul out the adjectives and relive the thrills of each par and birdie. Just wait until you're in the 19th hole. Up to that point, it's all just abstract numbers.

Survival at 21 Degrees

For the experienced golfer who shoots in the 80s and 90s, lofted woods can provide an inoculation against the dreaded double-bogey string. So says Craig Hatch, head professional at

Hart Ranch Golf Club in Rapid City, South Dakota. Every golfer makes double bogeys, even the pros. The real trick, Hatch believes, is to isolate them—one per nine would be nice. He counsels his students to learn the art of guiding their golf balls around the course on days when their golf swing doesn't feel quite right. By thinking clearly and making a few adjustments, you can use just two clubs to reliably cover the make-or-break distance range of 150 to 190 yards.

The two clubs championed by Hatch are the modern five-wood and seven-wood. By "modern," he means a five-wood with a loft angle of about 17 degrees and a seven-wood with a loft angle of about 21 degrees. (Prior to recent advancements in materials and head design, clubs stamped as five-woods or seven-woods had more extreme loft angles; without these "weak" loft angles, golfers would struggle to get the ball sufficiently airborne.) Hatch pleads with his golfers to get fitted for lofted woods and carry them at all times. He also encourages them to choke down on the five- and seven-woods to proactively alter carry distance on the shots they hit with these clubs.

"A typical 15-handicap male golfer hits his five-wood about 195 yards when he grips it in the standard fashion," Hatch begins. "Then, by choking down one inch, he can make the same swing and play confidently from about 185 yards. It's simple physics. Choke down two inches and that same swing will work from roughly 175 yards. For a shot of about 170 yards, the 21-degree seven-wood is the natural choice, assuming it is held normally. Choke down on the seven-wood one inch to cover the 160-yard distance and two inches to cover the 150-yard distance."

If this is such a shrewd maneuver, why don't more golfers discover it on their own? Hatch says the crafty players do. But these are golfers who are willing to admit their weaknesses and forgo use of the lower irons—especially on off days. "Most sets come with three-iron, four-iron, five-iron, so typical golfers feel it's their duty, basically, to use them. They also get skittish about choking down—the grip feels smaller in their hands and they have to adjust their stance to get closer to the ball. But, hey, they've got to do exactly that on an uneven lie, when the ball is above their feet, so what's the big deal?"

On a well-marked practice range, spend twenty minutes some day hitting five-woods and seven-woods in this crucial 150- to 200-yard "window." Make the same, solid swing every time and note the change in carry distance you produce by choking down various amounts. Depending on a player's size and strength, the distances will vary somewhat, but a great number of approach shots on par-4s, layup shots (and even drives) on par-5s, or tee shots on par-3 holes will fall into this yardage range.

"The lofted woods are the easiest-swinging clubs in the bag," Hatch counsels. "If you know how to use them creatively, you can still score well on a day when your full swing feels less than tip-top."

Take It Low by Beating Tension

The typical player who shoots 90 or better is too good at one aspect of golf, says the Orlando-based author and sports psychologist Patrick Cohn: "Keeping track of his score in his head." On days when the first nine to 12 holes are going especially well—in other words, the player in question is "taking it low"—that running tabulation leads to counterproductive tension. Cohn, an adviser to touring pros who has published a book on this very subject, has some dos and don'ts for players of all levels when they're shooting better than their average.

1. Don't keep track of your score; just play the round shot by shot. And by all means don't start wondering when the "blowup hole" or the "big number" is going to strike.

2. Avoid even positive "what if" scenarios that relate to score: "A golfer who stands over an iron shot on the 15th hole and thinks, 'If I can just get this on and two-putt, I'll be able to bogey in and still shoot 85,' usually hits a poorer shot than he would hit with an undistracted thought process," explains Cohn.

3. Keep challenging yourself. "What you don't want to do is go into a protect mode," Cohn says. "If you started out with a specific game plan that called for a conservative shot at a certain point, that's fine, but don't force that sort of approach based on how you stand in relation to par. You're better off getting a little bolder and challenging yourself to make birdies."

4. "Throw away generalizations." According to Cohn, it's psychologically unproductive even to say to yourself, "I'm on a hot streak,' or "I'm on a roll." That coin has an obvious flip side, which is that the "streak" or the "roll" eventually must end. "When you hear yourself starting to think in those terms," Cohn says, "go the other way and get more specific. Check the wind one extra time, double-count the yardage, pick out more exact targets. Treat the next shot like it's the only shot you're going to hit."

Streetwise Tips for Yardage and Clubbing

All day on the golf course, tournament golfers check yardage and make adjustments. Here are some of the basics of those adjustments, plus some real golf club selection advice, courtesy of Matt Abramavicius, of Marengo Ridge Golf Club, Marengo, Illinois.

▶ When playing to a very large green, you could hit as many as three different irons and still be on. Know for certain whether a yardage on a sprinkler head or colored fairway marker is to the front or center of each green.

▶ Playing uphill, take one extra club for every 10 to 15 feet of elevation change. Take one fewer club for every 10 to 15 feet you are playing downhill.

▶ Take one extra club for every eight miles per hour of head wind, one fewer club for every eight miles per hour of wind at your back.

▶ On par-4s of 325 yards or less, driver is probably an unwise club to hit off the tee. "When the architect gives you that short a hole, he's probably got some serious trouble in store for the player who hits driver and goes even a little off-line," says Matt.

▶ Don't base all your club selections on making a square, solid hit. "If you hit five out of 10 of your seven-iron shots on the toe or heel or fat or thin, that's five that won't fly their full distance," says Abramavicius. "Adjust down to the six-iron when there's no water or out-of-bounds behind the green and you have a sense—due to the lie, or whatever—that you might not catch this one full."

Make Par on Par-5s by Laying up Expertly

Listen to someone who usually shoots in the high 80s describe the thrilling 81 he just shot and you won't hear much about his second shots on the par-5s. To golf instructor Phil Keenan of Capital City Country Club in Cumming, Georgia, that's the sign of a blind spot. "Most golfers are too nonchalant about the second shot on a par-5," says Keenan, "unless it's a relatively short hole that they feel they can reach in two." Keenan claims we would all do a better of job of scoring and course management if we got better focused on the layup shot of a typical par-5 hole.

Here are Keenan's tips for leveraging the layup shot into lower scores. For starters, a golfer should understand what yardage (within the 80- to 125-yard range) he feels "most dangerous" from. Ask yourself: Do you simply love hitting your sand wedge or "gap" wedge with a full swing from 105 to 110 yards out? If so, that's the spot you'll want your par-5 layup coming to rest—not 25 yards closer, where you'll have to either switch clubs or else play a shot with less than a normal swing. "Planning your layups to stop in the 100 to 115 range has the advantage of keeping you away from the hazards and tightened landing areas that a typical par-5 will give you as you get closer to the green," says Keenan.

Assuming you've hit a decent drive, pick a club you feel comfortable with, Keenan advises, and visually define your layup target. It may help to "see" a very large green with a flagstick in the area you're headed for. Assess the green site and pin position to figure the ideal angle for your third shot, then make a normal, solid swing, focusing on direction and solid, center-of-the–club face contact. Above all, don't make an uncommitted, tentative swing. You've already planned conservatively, so feel free to execute aggressively.

Chapter 15

Read Greens Correctly

Understand the Speed Laws of Putting

A golf lifetime is spent trying to attune your brain and your hands to the pace and speed of the many and various putts you encounter. There's no other choice but to take them case by case, but Craig Farnsworth, a Colorado-based eye doctor–turned–sports vision specialist who has written two books on putting, would have you bear in mind four basic rules of speed and pace on the putting green.

1. Most putts have three separate speed zones: the initial burst, the basic rolling speed, and the braking speed. You have to try to visualize all three to hit any kind of lengthy putt with the right force.

2. Putts break the least when they're going their fastest and break the most when traveling their slowest. (Exception would be if there is a huge mound or ridge at the beginning of a putt and level ground near the hole.)

3. On fast greens, your putt travels slowly for most of its length, losing energy gradually; on slow greens, your putt travels quickly for most of its length, losing energy and speed in a short segment at the end.

4. Most side-breaking putts (especially on slick greens) have an "interstate highway" effect. For example, on a right-to-left breaker, you could get it going quickly toward the hole in the "left lane," more slowly in the middle lane, and slowest down the right lane. The more speed, the less break the putt will take and the less break you should play.

Count Paces, Visualize, and Predict Every Putt

Where tee-to-green yardages are concerned, guesswork and eyeballing are giving way to precise measurement. From sprinkler heads to yardage books to GPS computers on golf carts, golfers find themselves punctually informed that they have 168 yards to the front, 174 to the flag.

And it's high time we carried this over to the putting green. By consensus, today's teaching professionals agree that pacing off your chips and putts and knowing how many feet they measure is a great habit to get into. But pacing and counting is just the start; here's the routine teachers suggest, if you want to avoid three-putts and "make more than your share."

Anywhere from seven or eight feet and higher, pace off the distance of your putt and convert it from yards to feet. You'll not only come up with a helpful number, you'll have seen the length of your putt and noticed any bumps or dips along the way. (After several rounds of doing this, you should become fairly good at estimating before you actually pace and count—but don't rely on the estimate.)

"Load" that distance information into your thoughts and weigh it against such factors as slope (up or down), speed of the greens, even wind. If you acknowledge the fact that you have a 22-foot level putt on the first green, when you face an 18-foot level putt on the third green, you can then say to your-self: "Same force as I gave the putt on number 1." These little cues are a far sight better than standing there with no point of reference for how to swing.

Visualize every putt you hit going in, and visualize the roll you expect from everyone else's putts. Guess how hard a stroke Joe is going to make on his breaking 15-footer, and predict visually how it will travel. Putting is extremely visual, and this is great visual practice.

How (and When) to Read a Putt in Segments

One of the most common mistakes in putting is to read a putt as downhill and then leave it short. Usually what happens is that your downhill putt leveled out near the hole and became a flat putt. The lesson from this is to read some of your longer putts in sections or segments, keeping these fundamentals in mind:

1. Facing a putt that starts out level but goes upslope at the end, you have to previsualize the ball decelerating at a faster than normal rate. That putt has two separate

reasons for slowing down, so be sure and run a movie of it in your mind with the ball carrying more zip into the final segment than it would if it were level all the way. With correct visualization, you should be able to strike it with sufficient force to get it to the hole.

2. On a putt that starts out level, then turns downhill, do the opposite. This putt won't sprint, then jog, then walk; it will jog most of the way, then briefly walk before falling. So visualize it maintaining its basic pace and speed for almost its entire length.

3. Consider two 30-footers with the same amount of sidesloping dropoff—except in one of them that side-slope is in the first 10 feet and in the other it comes in the last 10 feet. You might play one foot of break for the first one and three feet of break for the second one. Why? Because a ball that is slowing down will be much more influenced by sideslope than a ball just coming off the club face and carrying its maximum speed.

This visualization work can be made easier, according to Richard Sayers, of Anchorage Golf Club, in Alaska, if you respond to the requirement of additional speed (such as situation number 1 calls for) not by telling yourself to hit the ball harder to the hole's actual location but by mentally "moving" the cup several feet past its actual location and putting to that imaginary cup. Likewise, to deal with a putt like the one in situation number 2, you might mentally move the cup a few feet closer to you.

Plumb-bobbing a Putt: What It Can and Can't Do

A golfer on the green used to look like he knew his stuff when he stood behind his ball with one eye shut, looking toward the cup and holding his putter pinched between thumb and forefinger, dangling downward. Here is why putting gurus like former U.S. Senior Amateur champion Gene Andrews and Dave Pelz have discredited the whole plumb-bobbing process.

Picture yourself on a long plank of wood with a stripe down the center of it holding an actual carpenter's plumb-bob in your hand. You hold this weighted string in front of you, closing one eye and lining the bottom of the string up with the stripe in the middle of the board.

Now, imagine that one long edge of the plank slowly rises four inches. You keep your balance, your hand and head don't move, and what happens? The bottom of the string now lines up near the left edge of the board, about four inches from the stripe. That, folks, is how plumb-bobbing a putt is supposed to work. Problems are manifold. The two most pressing are (a) The ground doesn't tilt uniformly, the way the plank does; and (b) your putter shaft tends to deviate from true plumb, because of the head and how it's attached. Andrews even pointed out that, because your dominant eye is not in the center of your head, at least one more inch of error gets introduced.

How can your putter shaft help with alignment and green reading? For one thing, it can create a temporary line finder between the hole and the ball. Hold it in that position, either hanging style or the way you would hold a sword, and examine the line for specs and spots that you can use as landmarks as you complete your prestroke alignment. Putting guru Craig Farnsworth even suggests you paint your putter shaft white so that it leaves an afterimage when you pull it away. For the next four or five seconds, you'll see a stripe of darkness dead along the path of your ball to the hole. If your putt is straight, just step in and hit it along that line.

Read a Green's Dominant Features (from Afar)

You've hit a nice approach shot on a tough par-4 or a nifty tee shot on a par-3, and you start walking toward the green. If your buddy starts asking you about pro football or a recent movie, David Lawrence wants you to answer while keeping your eyes on the green ahead. Lawrence, of Brentwood Golf and Country Club in White Lake, Michigan, says it's "often too late" when you are up at a green to appreciate its dominant features and understand how they will affect the speed, break, and even grain of your putt. So when you're on the tee of a par-3 or the approach area of a longer hole—this is especially true on downhill holes—do the following:

▶ Scope out the general lay of the land, looking for high ground and low ground to the sides of the green. "Think of water runoff," advises Lawrence. "The course builder will always create a runoff pattern, and your ball will naturally be influenced by those angles and directions."

▶ Examine the mounds immediately beside the green. These features will also direct water and, therefore, the break of your putt.

▶ Look at the swales and hogbacks on the green itself. "You'll see them when you're actually on the putting surface, but their relative size might be hard to appreciate due to the lack of perspective," says Lawrence.

To be sure, many greens have subtle twists and breaks that only affect putts rolling directly through and over them. But dominant features like hills, mounds, and depressions have an overall influence that will come into play time after time. Scope these out first, and begin doing it as soon as you can.

The Latest Pelz Breakthrough: True Break Angle

The innovative research conducted by former NASA engineer Dave Pelz in the area of putting and short game only grows in renown, making it impossible to lay out putting advice in a collection of this type without including at least one pure Pelz concept. In his lectures and writings of the past year or two, Pelz's most compelling bullet point has concerned what he calls "true break angle." It's a concept most people find astounding, and astoundingly simple, at the same time.

Think of any 20-footer you've recently faced that you read as having two feet of break. Ask yourself this question: Did I form a mental picture of the ball tracking along a curve to a point two feet outside the straight line between the cup and my starting point? Most people would say yes, and so far they're okay.

Next question: Did I address my ball with the face of my putter pointed toward the "apex," to use Pelz's term, of that curve? Was my basic intention to start the ball toward that apex point? If you said yes, you're part of the misguided masses.

That's because any ball that rolls over sidesloping ground is going to be steadily pulled off its original course *toward* some apex point. On the first couple of rolls, that pulling is minimal, due to initial speed. But after four or five revolutions, the ball has yielded to gravity's pull quite significantly. This being the case, the apex point—two feet off straight-and-narrow—is really a compromise point. By definition, it has to lie *between* the straight line and *some other* line. That other line is the line, Pelz tells us, of the "actual break angle." And any golfer who sinks this putt after rolling it on a reasonable pace would have to have started it on that actual break angle line. On a 20-footer that actually breaks two feet, that line, stretched out to a spot even with the hole, is more like six to 10 feet away from dead straight, not two feet.

So how do all the average golfers who don't understand this concept end up getting our 20-footers with two feet of break anywhere near the hole? We unconsciously pull or push all these putts. Our brains, Pelz explains, make up for the initial error by yanking or pushing the ball far outside the apex point. The result is a putt that never really had a chance but doesn't make us look like we've never been on a golf course before. That said, it's not a scientifically accurate way to approach breaking putts, and it explains a lot of our confusion, not to mention our three-putts.

Finish Your Reading with a Glance at the Grain

"If the grass is shiny, your putt is with the grain," says Shaun Kalos, of the Wigwam Resort Golf Course, Litchfield Park, Arizona. "If the grass is dull, you're going against it."

Reading the grain of a putt can be just that simple for cognoscenti who spend lots of time on Sunbelt greens that feature thickbladed bermuda grass. In places like Arizona, pros like Kalos can detect grain direction with a quick glance. Most amateur golfers assess their putts for slope first, then think about grain as a final factor. Kalos advises players who aren't used to reading grain to remember the following points:

▶ At some courses, there is a land feature (mountains, valleys, bodies of water) toward which all putts will be inclined to roll. Ask a local about this sometime before beginning your round.

▶ Absent a predominant tendency like that, remember that the grain of a green can many times be toward the setting sun and/or down the direction that water runs off. If the runoff direction is toward sunset, that's a dead lock to be the grain.

▶ The "shiny with, dull against" test is generally most reliable, but bear in mind that some of your putts will be crossgrain, not directly up or down.

▶ One other prime checkpoint for grain is the cup. "Look for the side of the hole with the blades leaning in," advises Kalos. The direction of that lean is the grain.

Once you know a green's grain, remember to allow for a little more or less break (or more or less speed) depending whether you're putting with it or against it. "Grain won't factor in at the beginning of a longer putt, when you've got the ball going at a good pace," concluded Kalos, "but as that putt slows down, grain will take its effect."

Chapter 16

Strokes to Sink More Putts

Thumbs Down Can Mean Thumbs Up for Your Putting

The globe-trotting Australian golf coach Peter Croker is best known for his full-swing concepts, which *Golf Digest* featured on its cover as the "Swing for the Future." But Croker studies the short game just as closely as the power game. He has originated an unusual-sounding putting tip that some of his students swear by.

Especially on straight putts from inside eight feet, "Stick your thumbs in the bottom of the hole," Croker urges. There isn't much more to the tip than that simple directive, which is actually a "feel cue" that sets off a series of correct movements for straight, solid putting. To try this tip, grip your putter with your thumbs resting on the front, flat surface of the handle. Find a relatively level, straight putt of about six or seven feet, and begin your stroke by moving the putter back freely and naturally, keeping the wrists unbent and using only your shoulders to hinge the stroke. As the arms reach the end of the backstroke, think only of dipping the tips of your thumbs in the bottom of the cup.

"That thought will give you an unwavering, nondecelerating forward stroke of the correct length—no off-line twisting of the hands or putter head—every time," Croker promises. Naturally, on breaking putts, you simply adjust the cue by mentally moving the "cup" where you'll be dipping those thumbs to one side or the other.

Don't Fight Your Stroke Tempo, Just Vary the Length

Several well-known experiments, including one conducted by golf researcher Gene Andrews, have shown that experienced golfers naturally stick to a surprisingly consistent putting-stroke tempo. Andrews, a U.S. Senior Amateur champion-turned–training guru, confirms that the time it takes any given pro or seasoned amateur to go from takeaway to impact won't change, whether the putt is four feet downhill or 40 feet uphill. Andrews went on to base all his teaching ideas on this premise, although he took the idea farther than most people—even true golf nuts— would probably take it.

He affixed a yardstick to his living room carpet, placed a metronome next to it, then ran a thick band of tape 40 feet down the carpet. Hitting putt after putt, he located a point on the yardstick—say 15 inches—that corresponded to a point out on the length of tape—say, 20 feet. Every putt started with the first metronome click and ended, at impact, with the second.

This unforced consistency of stroke tempo isolated length of backswing as Andrews's only variable.

Adapt this information to your own putting practice by setting up four or five balls on a flat section of a practice putting green. Trusting that your tempo will stay the same, hit one ball with a six-inch backswing, one with a nine-inch backswing, and one with a 12-inch backswing. Make a mental note of how far the balls rolled, then repeat the exercise one more time. Practice putting as you normally would after that, focusing now and then on your length of backswing and how much roll results from the various swing lengths. Finish by hitting ten or fifteen putts in the 15- to 35-foot range. Your control of the putter head and your ability to lag the ball close to the hole should be noticeably better than before.

Improve Your Skill at "Makeable Breakers"

From where your ball marker sits on the green to the nearest point along the edge of the hole is five feet exactly. You've been waiting your turn to putt, psyching yourself up to stroke a five-footer that you expect will be dead straight. Then the course's wisest and most respected caddie walks by and tells you the putt breaks five inches left to right.

Amazing but true golf fact: The ball marker didn't move and the hole didn't move, but your putt just got longer. Why? Because your ball is no longer destined to follow the shortest distance between two points: the straight line.

"It's also not going to go in by crossing that closest point along the hole's edge," points out Johnny Budwine, of Brick

Landing Plantation in Ocean Isle Beach, North Carolina. The mindset and commitment you need to make breaking putts is demanding, so Budwine gives his students commonsense advice and a favorite drill to help them along the way. We all struggle a bit with putts that traverse huge mounds and swales, but we need to have confidence on "makeable breakers." One common mistake on breaking putts is to actually "help" the break, meaning pull your putt to the left on a right-to-lefter and push it to the right on a left-to-right breaker.

Here's Budwine's pet drill for training yourself to commit to the initial line of a breaking putt: Lay a steel-shafted three-iron on the practice putting green and lightly slide the heel of your putter along the three-iron's shaft so that you can feel (and perhaps ever hear) your putter heel hitting the "steps" of the shaft. Then set up over a breaking six-foot putt with the three-iron shaft aligned perfectly parallel to the line the ball needs to travel to go in. Drop several balls and, dragging them over one at a time, stroke them on a natural pace with the heel of your putter rubbing along the shaft steps. "The point of this drill," says Budwine, "is to understand that every putt you ever stroke is a straight putt"—a straight putt that needs an unwavering stroke of the putter head to get where it needs to go. "It won't always be a straight line all the way to the hole," Budwine says, "but it's always a straight putt to the target right or left of the hole that you've picked out."

Time to Rethink Your Putter Grip Style?

A year or two ago, PGA Tour pro Chris Dimarco was hitting fairways, hitting greens . . . and missing cuts. Desperate for better putting, Dimarco tried an experimental "claw" grip that worked wonders. It's difficult to describe this technique in words, except to say that it begins with both of Dimarco's hands on the club normally. Then the right hand comes off, flips over (as though Dimarco were looking at his wristwatch) and reattaches to the putter handle in a light, fingers-only pinch. This is done to make the left hand dominate the stroke, which has resulted in a smoother, more controlled and consistent stroking action for this particular tour player.

Assuming your own putting woes can be cured via less extreme grip experiments, here are some possibilities, with help from Josh McBroom, who teaches at Northwood Golf and Country Club in Shreveport, Louisiana.

1. Switch to "cross-handed": For the righty golfer, that's left-hand low, right-hand high. While many tour players have tried this grip, Fred Couples is perhaps most recognizable for sticking with it. As with the Dimarco Variation, cross-handed putting makes the pulling hand, and the hand connected to the "front" shoulder, dominant. For many golfers this has a steadying effect.

2. Lay your right finger down the back of the shaft. "Players who use this grip successfully use that finger just to help them key into the line of the putt," says McBroom. In other words, they don't break their right wrist and push on the shaft with the extended right finger.

3. For the right-handed golfer, putting lefty. "Notah Begay is a tour player whose putter can be used from either side," says McBroom. Begay putts lefty some of the time, righty some of the time, always setting up so that

a breaking putt breaks right to left, the easier curving direction to judge and handle.

And if things really get desperate, you know there's always the Dimarco Claw to resort to.

Play Speedy Downhillers with the Usually Taboo Toe

The putter inches back warily on its takeaway stroke, floats forward, contacts the ball, and sends it merrily on its downhill way, far past the hole. "I didn't even hit that, I just tapped it," moans the golfer now facing the 15-foot comebacker. Yes, but he tapped it with the center of his putter blade, just as you're (usually) supposed to do. Matt Abramavicius, of Marengo Ridge Country Club in Marengo, Illinois, would have advised this player to break the center-contact rule in this slippery instance.

"On a very fast downhill putt, you still want to move the putter head with enough authority to direct the ball's path," says Abramavicius. "By playing the ball out toward the toe of your blade, you can do that and still take a lot of the energy out of the impact." Once that testy putt is behind you, the pro advises, go right back to striking your putts on the sweet spot.

Chapter 17

Smart Ways to Practice

New Set? New Season? Find a Spot to Measure Your Clubs' Yardages

That a golfer would want to know how far his shots fly with the various woods and irons is a matter of common sense. But seasoned instructors all agree there's a difference between wanting to know, thinking you do know, and doing what's necessary to find out. Here is their consensus recipe for learning which yardages to play your various clubs from.

1. Bring your wedges to a football field. "Getting out of the golf setting, whether it's a range or a course, really helps you understand pure carry distance of your scoring clubs—the wedges, nine-iron, even eight-iron," says David Lawrence, of Brentwood Golf and Country Club in White Lake, Michigan. "Hit wedge shots on a flat field back and forth a couple of times and pace off the yardage until you find a basic average for each club."

2. Hit mid-irons from the right spot on the range. A big "150" or "175" sign on a typical driving range may be rather casually sited. Ask the teaching pro at your range whether the signs are correct, including which section of the tee area they are measured from. Hit five shots with each of your mid-irons and take the average, not the longest, as your "readout." If possible, try to do this off a grass surface, not a mat (which will distort the distances), and not a wooden tee, either.

3. Measure the driver and three-wood with an extra grain of salt. Does it matter how long your best bombs with the driver and three-wood measure? Sure it does; any golfer would want to know how much raw power he or she is packing. But when you're candidly assessing the carry distance of these clubs, do it on the assumption you're about to play a very long par-3. Figure out whether your three-wood couldn't fit the bill on a 205-yard 3-par. See if a 220-yard par-3 (and there are more of them being built than ever these days) doesn't have room for your driver, especially if you choke down an inch. Real-golfer studies by course designer William Amick have shown that most average golfers could readily play these "big" clubs on par-3s in that distance range.

Follow the Stripe on Practice Putts to See Break, Smooth the Stroke

This is an old, yet little-known tour-pro exercise. To try it yourself, take several striped range balls to a practice green and spend 15 or 20 minutes hitting long, short, straight, and break-ing putts. Start by placing a few of your striped balls on a level area with the stripe appearing directly on top of each ball. Stroke each ball hard enough to roll it between five and 10 feet. As it rolls, check the stripe to see if it remains visible on "top" of the ball. If it does, then your stroke and the impact of your putt is true and solid. If the stripe appears to veer to the side and fall off the top of the ball, either you've "cut" or you've "hooked" the putt, meaning your putter's face has come in at an oblique angle. This type of impact is not desirable, throwing off both the direction and the pace of your putts. Continue put-ting on this level surface until you can keep the stripe on the top or near it with every putt.

The other great use of the striped-ball drill is its visual enhancement of side-to-side break. As a matter of plain fact, we all know that a breaking putt causes our golf ball to cease rolling on its original circumference (marked by the stripe) and "fall" or roll sideways in the direction of the break. But until you see it dramatized by the veering of the ball stripe as the putt takes its break, you may not truly realize the extent to which break putt takes speed out of a putt, or how necessary it is to set up your breaking putts so they enter the hole some-where beside the "front door."

Practice Post-Round, and Work on Your Weaknesses

This next bit of hardheaded advice and comment comes not from a full-time teaching pro but rather from golf's closest equiv-alent, a pro-tour caddie. Bob Ming, the professional caddie in question, is also a computer maven who has developed golf-performance software specifically for use by tournament players. When it comes to post-round practice sessions, Ming has an odd comment to make about following a tour pro's example.

"Most touring pros you see hitting drivers after their round have actually driven the ball well that day," observes Ming. "The ones you see hitting middle irons have hit their middle irons well. They're reinforcing what's working because it's a satisfying experience. What they should be working on is the club or the shot that isn't performing."

The day after you play 18, go back over the round and count fairways missed and greens missed, advises Ming. Count your three-putts and take note of the putts you missed inside eight feet. ("Make from inside eight feet or we don't eat," is his memorable slogan for the pros he consults.) What you'll come up with is a priority list of what needs working on. "It's human nature to want to practice the shots that are going well," Ming says, "so don't deny yourself that pleasure. Just make sure you've put in some serious work on the trouble spots first."

On the Range, Simulate a Real Round

Average golfers often lament, "I hit the ball well on the driving range. Why can't I translate that to the golf course?" The problem with that concept is that on the range we all hit many poor shots along with the good ones. (We simply don't remember the poor shots, mostly because we don't have to find them and play them, but somewhat because we don't *want* to remember them.)

Instead of hitting long series of practice shots with one club and only recalling the ones that work out well, try a practice technique favored by California sports psychologist and trainer Glen Albaugh—we'll call it the simulated-round approach. Among Albaugh's clients who swear by this technique is PGA Tour standout Scott McCarron.

Here's the drill: Arrive at the range and spend some time hitting drivers, wedges, five-irons, or whichever clubs you please. After you're warmed up and satisfied with the repetition segment of your practice session, begin a "round." Choose a challenging golf course that you know well and hit a tee shot on the range to a target area that matches that course's first fairway. If you hit a poor drive, hit another, but tally that second ball in your "score" for the hole. Then hit the second shot that the selected hole calls for, once again to a visualized target that matches the real target on the course.

See how long a streak you can put together in which your first attempt at each drive, long approach, or short pitch succeeds. Don't rush between shots; instead, take your time and go through a preshot routine. You'll get a better sense of reality from this technique, along with more productive practice. In fact, it will be the kind of practice you actually *can* carry over to the golf course.

Pre-Round Putting Practice: No Eyes, All Feel

It is undeniably true that to putt accurately you have to be sharp visually, both as you read each putt's break and slope and as you attempt to align to your target and stay aligned while you're over the ball. Be that as it may, the all-important visual system should actually be down for much of your preround putting warmup. That's the opinion of Johnny Budwine, an innovative teaching pro at Brick Landing Plantation in Ocean Isle Beach, North Carolina. Here's what Budwine likes to see his students do before they head to the first tee.

1. Drop several balls on a quiet end of the practice putting green and—keeping a gentle grip on the putter—spend a few minutes putting these balls with your eyes firmly closed. "Putt them to no particular target," says Budwine. "Just feel how much of a stroke you're giving it, then observe how far the ball goes." With the round about to begin, Budwine explains, a feel-building drill such as this is much more valuable than working on mechanics.

2. Start stroking the ball toward a hole, still with your eyes closed. "Start as close in to the hole as necessary in order to sink a bunch of them," he says, "then move back as far as 18 feet, no farther." Closing your eyes, according to Budwine, prevents your head from *moving without any conscious reminder to keep it still.* When the head stays still and there's a lot of feel in the hands, the tendency to leave putts short is greatly reduced.

3. Finish out your pre-round putting practice however you wish, with three provisos: Stay mostly at a range of 20 feet and in; go back to eyes-closed practice if you start losing the feel you've been honing; just work on feel, not mechanics, and be aware of what the putter does when it's given a chance to swing freely.

Playing "Pullback" Is Fun Today, Stroke-Saving Tomorrow

During the golf season, club pros and teaching profession-als don't get much time away from their duties. But they do have a course and practice range right there when they get off work, plus coworkers who are as skilled and competitive as they are. The result is competitive practice, especially on the short game. It's an aspect of the golfing lifestyle that keeps handicaps down and boredom at bay. Josh McBroom, of Northwood Golf and Country Club in Shreveport, Louisiana, explains one example, the Putting Game "Pullback": Two play-ers or more each drop a ball on the putting green at tap-in range to start. They lengthen the putt by a couple of feet until one of them misses. Whoever misses has to pull his ball back a putter length and try from that distance. If he sinks it, they move to a new hole. If he misses, he continues pulling back a club length until he makes the putt. While the difficulty factor appears to rise, remember that these ever-lengthening putts roll on the same line each time, so that for a while they actually become increasingly makeable. "Eventually a guy is all the way across a huge green and out of range," says McBroom. At that point, the players make mental note of a nickels-and-dimes (or dollars) transfer and continue the game.

Once you get in the mood of competitive practice, the var-ious games can be adapted to different types of shots. In the evenings, McBroom and his mates play a 90-yard five-ball game with their sand wedges—"Set a price and the closest out of the five wins," he says. In the practice bunkers, they'll play a similar best-of-five game, one round from an easy lie, one from a downhill lie, one with the ball half buried.

"Sometimes there's money on the line," says McBroom, "more often it's the sheer competition that makes it interesting. Practice your short game this way and it doesn't feel like a chore. It's actually a good chance to feel pressure, which helps you really find the weaknesses in your game."

Running Through an Ideal Twenty-Minute Bunker Workout

Matt Carsey doesn't know too many golfers conscientious enough to ask this question, but when the query as to how a twenty-minute bunker practice session should be organized, this was Carsey's reply.

1. "Vary the distance on your shots one after the next," says Carsey. "Hit a short, high shot, then a longer, lower shot, then something in between." Repeat this cycle several times.

2. Just as you vary distance, vary the type of lie you play from. "Hit from a level lie, then move to an upslope lie, then try a few off a downslope," suggests Carsey, who works at Lakeview Golf Course in the town of Ralston, Nebraska. "And step on a few before you hit them." In other words, press the ball down with your foot slightly, to create the slightly buried condition you'll often encounter in real-life golf.

3. Experiment with open-face and square-face address angles. The former magnifies the "bounce" quality of your wedge's head design; the latter allows it to dig

more. Without trying to hit a ball any particular distance, see what a simple change in face angle will accomplish.

4. Vary backswing length, just making sure you never decelerate through impact.

And as you're concluding your practice session, Carsey suggests you hit five balls toward one or more target pins, then step out with your putter and see how many you can sink for an up-and-down sand save. "Unless you're a single-digit-handicapper, you probably won't get up and down with more than one of the five attempts," Carsey muses. "The lesson that teaches you is the importance of simply escaping over trying to hit it close."

How to Hone Your Driving Game on the Range

Two golfers pick out adjacent spots on the driving range and spill their jumbo buckets of striped balls. The Good Golfer starts his session with the wedge and works his way slowly through the irons, finally up to the woods, giving each club a fair workout. The Bad Golfer whips out his driver, rears back, and pounds ball number one down the range. Never changing clubs, he lets the Big Dog eat the remaining 79 practice balls. We who know better turn our heads in pity, aware we've witnessed ignorant golf practice in its purest form.

Okay, then, it's uncool to go to the range and pound drive after drive. But, let's be clear: The tee shot is not some marginal aspect of the game. Mike Bender, pro at Timicuan Golf and Country Club in Lake Mary, Florida, was asked where the tee shot should rank in a golfer's priority. "Driver," Bender replies, "is the most important club in the bag. The tour's all-time money list is not dominated by the great putters," he comments, and leaves it at that. Bender was then asked the pressing question: How does a golfer productively practice his driving game?

"The problem isn't that you go to the range and hit a lot of driver shots," says Bender, a winner of the *Golf Digest* 50 Best Teachers award. "The problem is that you do it without targets or goals or any way to evaluate the results." To correct that error, we should:

1. "Define a fairway on the range," in Bender's words. "Set a goal of putting so many balls out of ten in play, not blowing one ball past another."

2. "Have a consistent shape to your tee shots." Bender is one of those professionals who considers the straight-flying shot a myth. Most balls hit with the driver curve in some direction—what you want to see on the range is a consistent curve pattern.

3. "Watch the ball all the way," urges Bender. "See it in the air and see it land." Out on the golf course, the difference of five feet means rough, not fairway. On the range, we should remember those small differences and track our drives all the way through to finish. "On any shot," says Bender, a former PGA Tour player, "observe the whole flight. The ball takes off, it curves, it lands . . . the important thing is where it stops."

Chapter 18

Special Situations

Adjusting on the Fly: What You Can and Can't Do Mid-Round

To mentally steer the day's new round toward success, scratch golfers have been known to whisper: "Make the first birdie before you make a bogey." Average golfers can translate that to: "Make a par before you make the first double-bogey." It's a surprisingly effective little axiom, but some days the demons come out early and enthusiastically. Depending which sector of your game is going off-kilter, here, courtesy of Walter Hix III (Wildhawk Golf Club, Sacramento, California) and several other interviewed pros, are some intra-round adjustments to put into motion.

▶ Putts left way short: Stroke one or two practice putts on a green you've just played, looking at the hole (not the ball) as you make the stroke. These "peekaboo" putts should roll a much more appropriate distance than your actual putts.

▶ Putts significantly off-line: Play less break; in fact, assume every putt is straight and hit them at the hole.

▶ Hitting iron shots thin or fat: "Start with ball position," advises Hix. "Get your ball positioned just left of center for the irons and just off (perhaps a little more than just off) the left heel for the woods."

▶ Slicing, hooking, pushing, pulling: "Avoid mechanical adjustments," says Hix, or you're likely to end up having no idea where the ball is going. "Make strategic adjustments only," he advises. "Aim left if you're slicing, aim right if you're hooking, and use less club when you're around water or another severe hazard." In general, work your strategy so that any error costs you one stroke instead of two or more.

How "B" and "C" Players Help Their Scramble Teams Win

With corporate and charity golf outings now so popular, the four-man "scramble" can sometimes feel like the basic format of play. Love it or merely tolerate it, the scramble game has an intriguing strategy all its own—and some attractive prizes for the winners. With help from Travis Guisinger, a pro at Noble Hawk Golf Links in Kendalville, Indiana, we've laid down advice on how to return from your next scramble with new shiny hardware.

1. Birdies are essential to a high finish, but you won't help your team with go-for-broke shots. "Especially if you have average skill, which would make you the B or C man on the team, you'll help most by playing decent, solid shots," says Guisinger. This is particularly true of the early holes, when avoiding bogey is paramount.

2. Follow your captain's guidance. When the A player asks you to putt first, or to pick up what you feel to be the

best drive of the four and put it back in your pocket, don't quibble.

3. "Be careful not to overswing," warns Guisinger. "You can be aggressive, but don't try what's out of your range." When the team has a tee shot in the fairway beyond where you can reach, treat your turn to drive as helpful practice.

4. Choose your own clubs and shape your own shots. When the A player takes a seven-iron and flies his approach shot to a green that is open in the front but has water behind and right, feel free to take your five-iron and hit a run-up that bounces 20 yards in front and rolls on. All four of you are trying to help the team make birdie, but you shouldn't play in lockstep.

5. On the greens, get your putts to the hole. This is one area where your style of play should indeed adjust. All putts in a scramble have to reach the cup or roll a few feet past, otherwise they do the team no good. Even if your putt doesn't drop, by reaching the hole it will at least show your next teammate the correct line and the break.

The Endurance Game: Playing Four or Five Days in a Row

Visit the third or fourth round of any big member-guest tournament and you'll hear weekend golfers remarking at the effort it takes to play 18 holes of golf—especially in a competitive tournament—that many days in a row. The other occasion for weekend players to stretch their golfing out to four or five consecutive days is on a golf-buddy vacation to Myrtle Beach, Phoenix, or some other wintertime golf mecca.

According to Sean Sundra, of Stonebridge Golf Club in Monroe, North Carolina, fatigue may work against you slightly, but playing on many consecutive days can also produce some of your best golf. Here's how to make that happen:

▶ Warm up on the range as you normally would, but don't go in for any lengthy and tiring ball-beating sessions. Devote more than the usual amount of swings to chips and pitches. And stretch out in the morning and evening as much as possible.

▶ Bring a tube of muscle balm to rub on sore areas, and keep adhesive tape handy in case blisters begin to appear on your hands. "Don't apply any tape as a preventative measure," Sundra warns, "because the tape itself can cause abrasions to the skin it rubs against."

▶ Get to bed early ("Don't be the last guy at the stag party, whatever you do," he says) and eat multiple small meals instead of a heavy breakfast and lunch. Also, carry water and keep fully hydrated throughout the round.

▶ Take a positive attitude toward all the repetitions. "Your feel on approach shots and the short game should definitely improve as the rounds go on," says Sundra, even more so if you're playing the same course repeatedly.

Once you're off the course, conserve energy. Paddle around in the hotel pool but don't knock yourself out on the fitness center treadmill. You can keep mentally fresh by taking your mind off golf with a movie or a card game in the evening.

Get a Competitive Edge in the Rain

Floods and hurricanes will close down any golf course, but your office-tournament match probably won't be canceled by a steady, soaking rain. Some golfers are disheartened by rainy conditions, but others take an odd pleasure in employing all the little rain-beating tricks available. Here's a rainy-day list of effective moisture-beating tactics.

▶ Arrive at the course with several dry towels in a sealed plastic bag; take a new one out every four or five holes. Dry the grip of the club you're using next, then dry your hands fully, not just the palms.

▶ Break out the umbrella, rain jacket, and rain pants as soon as they're needed. Don't let pants, socks, and shirt get wet on a day they're unlikely to dry.

▶ Look in a full-line golf store for specially made rain gloves. They are made of cotton instead of synthetic leather and won't slip on the grip even when they're completely wet.

▶ Keep a rain hood over your clubs and zip it up between shots. If the wind is light, keep your umbrella over your clubs while playing a shot.

▶ If the bottom of the bag gets standing water in it, slide tees into the vent holes of your grip caps. This will keep the knob of each club above the water line.

▶ Take full advantage of Rule 25 covering casual water on the rough and fairway. "Any accumulation of water which is visible" constitutes casual water, and most players look at the top of their shoe heel to determine "visible." You drop without penalty, no nearer the hole, at the closest spot that affords relief.

Handling the Switch from Fast to Slow
Greens (and Back Again)

If you play a wide variety of courses locally—and especially if you take your clubs on airplanes to play in different geographic regions—you will end up putting on slow greens one day, fast greens a few days later, or vice versa. Someone new to the game of golf who saw a page of advice devoted to this problem might scratch the head (as in, how hard could *that* be?).

Barry Walters, a member of the pro staff at the Members Club at St. James Plantation, Southport, North Carolina, breaks the problem down.

"You'll do a lot better in these situations if you're in the habit of always practicing long to short," says Walters. "On any practice putting green, start out at 30 feet, then go to 25, then 20, 15, five." Moving from far to near, logic would dictate, means getting your ball progressively closer to the hole through the practice session. A definite confidence booster and "the right way to get your feel for the speed," says Walters.

If the early putts from long range simply cannot get close, Walters offers what amounts to a dirty trick: looking at the hole as you putt. Anyone who's tried this (and whose eye-hand coordination is at least half decent) will tell you it can be effective enough right off the bat to almost feel like cheating. "It's called a 'feel' for the distance," says Walters wryly, "but you get that feel through your eyes."

For some golfers, there is a snob factor in going from one's regular club, with its politically correct slick greens, to some equally nice facility that happens to have greens on the slow side. "I just can't bring myself to hit it hard enough to get there," says the snobby golfer. Walters responds with advice straight from a fairy tale. "Before each putt, do the Goldilocks drill," he says. "Make one practice stroke that you know is too hard (like Papa Bear's mattress) and one that you know is too soft (like Mama Bear's). Then step up to the ball and put your best Baby Bear stroke on it." With any luck, that one will be just right.

Back on the Tee: How to Return from a Long Layoff

The astronaut returning from six months in the space station, the surgical patient finally finished rehabbing a knee, and the golfer who simply stashed his clubs for a season all enjoy a similar opportunity, says the noted *Golf Digest* Schools instructor Bob Lennon. "They've got a chance to assess their golf game from a fresh perspective and rebuild using solid fundamentals."

If you someday find yourself in this situation, says Lennon, who is based at Blue Heron Lakes Golf Club in Cologne, New Jersey, that's the time to approach a skilled and enthusiastic teacher who will deploy his video equipment, his club-fitting skills, and a logical series of refresher lessons to set you on a new road to golf performance. Be particularly open to buying at least two or three new custom-built golf clubs. It's highly possible that your old bad habits were simply compensating moves to make up for a shaft flex, a lie angle, or a head design that didn't reward your purest and most athletic swing motions.

If you're coming back from a layoff without the firsthand guidance of an instructor, Lennon suggests the following tactics:

▶   Spend your first golf session with just a pitching wedge or a nine-iron in hand. Chip and pitch a large bucket of range balls, not worrying about your accuracy to any particular target.

▶   Find a mirror (most golf learning centers have them) and get in the habit of standing in front of it while you make a series of swings, some slow-motion and some actual speed. Check yourself for sound setup fundamentals before the swings begin and sound impact fundamentals as you arrive at the bottom of your downswing. "Basically, you are looking for a straight line at impact between the ball, club head, left wrist, and left shoulder," says Lennon.

▶   In the early going, spend time simply making rehearsal-type swings (with or without a golf club) in which your hips are actively rotating back and then through so that you feel well-balanced throughout and your body weight is noticeably going to the back foot, then evenly spread, then finishing on the front foot.

Once out on the course, don't be too picky about what happens. "An experienced golfer coming back will probably notice a repeating shot pattern fairly soon in the round," says Lennon. "If that pattern is reasonably playable, stick with it for the day and worry about altering it on the practice range later."

Chapter 19

Tips on Equipment and Club Fitting

Red Flags from the Golf Bag:
Signs Your Clubs Don't Fit

June Staton is head professional at Cedarville Golf and Tennis Club, Old Brookville, New York, and one of the New York area's best-trained club fitters. She can't see into the golf bag of players she's never met, but Staton is experienced enough to present a bullet list of common swing flaws and ball-flight problems that often indicate misfit golf clubs. She prefaces that list with some basic common sense about the relationship between golf swing and golf club.

"The equipment you use affects your swing motion," says Staton. "Clubs that don't fit will throw you out of balance." If you spend time and money learning how to play this game, Staton would have you remember one thing: Instruction is based on having the clubs fit the golfer in the first place. "Sound instruction won't work," she warns, "if the clubs are far enough off from what they should be. The teacher will tell you a certain type of swing to make, you'll follow orders, and the ball won't go where it should. So you'll adjust and start making funny compensations to steer the ball back where you want it to go. But those compensations will cut down on your power, accuracy, and consistency."

So watch out for these signs:

Hitting on the toe: Lie angle of your irons may be too upright.

Reverse pivot: Your clubs may be too long or too heavy, or both.

Overly strong grip: Shaft flex too stiff; lie angle too flat.

Topping or thin hits: Shaft flex too stiff.

Incomplete follow-through (a.k.a. "blocking"): Shaft flex too whippy.

Remember, these are just examples and possibilities. The point is to have you rethink that axiom "It's not the arrow, it's the Indian," which is one of golf's most unenlightened, knee-jerk sayings. Repeat it only at the risk of making the same mistakes over and over, because even though your swing concept is sound, the clubs you are using won't let that sound swing do its work properly.

How to Know If Your Club Fitter Is Doing the Job Right

Golf clubs of different makes and models differ from each other in hard-to-spot ways. You can't see the lie angles of the irons; you can't, from the markings, tell much about shaft stiffness and flex points; and the loft angles on the woods don't tell you much, either, because of internal weighting patterns that offset or magnify the effects of simple loft angle. Even if golf equipment were standardized and fully labeled with specifications, you still wouldn't know which ones were ideal for you.

Thankfully, professional club fitting has come a long way in the past fifteen years. That said, most amateur golfers don't know whether they're getting the best that modern fitting has to offer. A careful survey of what's out there reveals the following fine points of club-fitting expertise and service. Make sure you're getting as full a menu of it as possible:

▶ Get fit outdoors, where the full flight of the ball can be observed.

▶ Expect your fitting to start with a check of your own irons on a flat sheet of plastic called a lie board. Your irons will be taped on the bottom (and often on the face, as well) to show whether the lie impact mark is correctly in the center of the sole and the ball impact mark is correctly in the center of the club face. If these marks are off, expect the fitter to test you with irons of a different lie angle.

▶ Look for a logical sequence of diagnostics, starting usually with iron lie and proceeding through shaft flex, flex point (high, low, mid), shaft length, head design (offset, non-offset, low-profile, etc.) driver loft, grip size, and so on.

▶ Most fittings aren't specifically golf lessons, but a skilled club fitter will be commenting knowledgeably on your swing form, letting you know whether it seems to be getting more natural and unforced—which is the goal—as the session proceeds.

▶   When a certain set of club specifications is finally recommended, a full-service fitting company will generally need
to send this data to its factory to have the club components
selected, prepared, and assembled. It's unlikely the set that's
right for you will be waiting back at the shop on the rack or in
a box. (You should, in fact, be able to order just a couple of the
irons and perhaps a driver, paying only for these few clubs, if
you so choose.)

It's natural to want a printout of your specifications, and
some companies will oblige. Others will resist, feeling the data
is hard-earned by the fitter's expertise and shouldn't rightfully
be passed on to some other club assembler. It's also likely the
fitting company will feel that the specifications can't be pre-
cisely replicated using the components manufactured by a different company.

Three-Putting Too Much?
"Get the Hang" of a New Putter

Teaching professionals naturally believe it is far better for a
struggling golfer to visit his lesson tee than to run to the golf
store and impulsively buy new equipment. That said, award-
winning instructor Sue Kaffenburgh, of Hyannis Golf Club in
Hyannis, Massachusetts, enthusiastically urges any golfer who
is putting poorly to switch to a new putter. Just make sure
you're armed with some knowledge when you do so—including these seldom-considered facts.

1.   A putter's design greatly influences your ability to align
     it correctly. "It's not a matter of the putter being well
     designed or poorly designed," says Kaffenburgh, "it's

all a matter of how your eyes and your brain react to the shape and markings of the putter." Years of tests with lasers reveal that one golfer can align on target with a blade-shaped putter, another does so with a mallet-style head. Some of us get thrown off our alignment by an offset hosel or neck, some of us improve our alignment due to this feature. The length of the putter head, its markings, even its color can strongly affect how well or poorly we align to our target.

2. A new putter "wakes up" our visual system and generally enhances performance. "Bear in mind that a streak of poor putting becomes strongly associated with the putter we're using," says Kaffenburgh. "You build up baggage, which a new putter helps you get rid of." If there is a putter-fitting expert in your area who uses the laser system for checking alignment, select your new putter design with his or her guidance. If there's no such resource, go to the rack and try out a dozen or so options. Work on level, straight putts in the five- to ten-foot range and identify the putter that looks most aligned to the hole when it is, indeed, properly aligned. A friend standing behind you along the target line is a great help in this experiment.

3. While weight and "head feel" are certainly important, the first non-alignment attribute to look for in a putter is whether it allows you to stand fairly upright and hang your arms naturally from your shoulders so that your hands end up comfortably in position to grip the handle. In other words, "get the hang" of your new putter,

Kaffenburgh advises, and start making a pro-style stroke that is all shoulders and arms, not hands and wrists.

An added bonus of following this last bit of advice is that you'll be able to practice your putting for a good length of time without getting tense and knotted up in the lower back. That practice, combined with a well-chosen new putter, will get you out of three-putt land and back into contention.

Addition by Subtraction: Weed Out Swing-Fouling Clubs

Ever noticed that if you try a friend's three-wood on the range and hit a poor shot with it, you'll almost always hit a better shot the second and third times you try? That's because every golf club has dynamic characteristics—stiffness, weight, loft angle—that an experienced golfer's brain, even on a couple of tries, can figure out and respond to via swing adjustments. Professional club fitters like Chris Aoki, of Harbour Pointe Golf Club in Mulkiteo, Washington, witness this phenomenon all day long as they shuttle test clubs in and out of their client's hands.

A similar occurrence happens within your own set of clubs, especially if every club in your bag wasn't custom-fitted for you by an expert. And it can lead to problems. Here's how:

"You stand on the first tee," explains Aoki, "and drive off with your three-wood, which we'll say has an offset head and a flexible shaft. Then, a few minutes later, you find yourself swinging your six-iron, which has a non-offset head and a stiff shaft. Unfortunately, your brain will still be thinking about the three-wood swing and how that three-wood shot went off-target—say, to the left of where you were aiming. That off-line flight triggered your brain to unconsciously identify certain adjustments, which you naturally make on your next swing. Trouble is, that adjusted swing will be made with a differently designed club, so it won't be appropriate."

What to do? First off, go through your bag with a critical eye and take out any club that you truly dislike the feel of. Such clubs are likely to cause problems not only when you actually hit them but when you go to hit the next shot—due to the adjustment syndrome. "On the positive side," says Aoki, "identify your two or three favorite clubs. They're your favorites because they fit your swing." You can take these clubs to a quality club fitter and find out more about them, with an eye toward buying more that feature the same "favorite club" characteristics. The ultimate goal: a bag full of clubs that are all your favorites.

Build Your Wedge Arsenal for Attacking as Well as Escaping

Assembling a wedge set that will arm you for every sort of birdie-making or par-saving opportunity is an easy exercise to begin. You start with a true greenside sand wedge possessing plenty of bounce angle and sole width:

"Something with about 55 or 56 degrees of loft is what you want for the wedge that'll get you safely out of greenside bunkers," says Barry Walters, of the Members Club at St. James in Southport, North Carolina. This club would generally have a bounce angle (the angle you see when you hold the club head at eye level—with the shaft plumb vertical—and look along the line from its leading edge to its trailing edge) of about eight degrees, more if necessary. Wedges of this type are thicker-soled than clubs made for grass lies. Some feature a flare or extension of the trailing edge called a flange.

After that, it's a matter of adding wedges with carry yardages that cover key distances from the fairway or rough off a relatively full swing.

"If your pitching wedge carries 130 yards from a good lie," Walters says, "you'll be looking for a sand wedge you can hit about 115 yards. Basically, you're looking to fill gaps." By that reasoning, if the sand wedge that flies 115 has 52 degrees of loft, you could test one out with about 55 degrees of loft to see if it flies 100-some yards with a normal swing.

This wedge may seem redundant, given how close it is in loft to your easy-out club, but the difference is in the sole configuration. A club that rides nicely into sand and emerges easily from it will tend to fight the turf and lead to thin or fat shots. "This wedge needs to nip the ball and the turf," Walters points out, "not bounce along it."

This brings your sand wedge count to three, which is all the weekend golfer wishing to observe golf's fourteen-club limit can generally afford to carry. Adding a 60-degree "lob" wedge will make it difficult to cover the other end of the distance spectrum—your fairway woods and a long iron or two. Golfers who do find room for a 60-degree wedge among their fourteen sticks tend to be capable of playing greenside bunker shots with a "compromise" sand wedge. By "compromise," we mean a club lofted in the 55-degree range with only moderate bounce and sole width. It takes a bit more talent (or perhaps practice) from sand to be able to use this club for greenside escapes, but if you can do it you get the advantage of adding that 60-degree wedge—good for lob shots and high-spin pitch shots—and still not giving anything up on the distance end of your set.

Build an Arsenal, Then Choose Fourteen

Rule 4-4, so famously breached by Ian Woosnam in the 2001 British Open, is the reason so many golfers go to the first tee with a maximum of fourteen clubs (including putter) in their bags. For others it's a mere matter of not wanting to haul an overly heavy golf bag around town. But just because you are only permitted to carry fourteen clubs doesn't mean you shouldn't own and use—on a rotating basis—as many as seventeen, eighteen, or even twenty. Here's how John Poole, head pro at Chester Valley Country Club in Malvern, Pennsylvania, would have you build your arsenal and then shuttle the most appropriate equipment into the bag for each round.

First, build your "sand," "gap," and "lob" wedge inventory up to four or five clubs, ranging from about 50 degrees to 60 degrees in loft angle. Identify the one or two wedges that work well from sand and determine through practice which one is best out of soft, fluffy, Florida-type sand and which is more effective from firmer, heavier sand. Then load up the bunker club that seems best suited to the course you're going to play. As for the other wedges—the ones you will generally play from fairway and rough—choose among them according to how many high-lob versus normal-height shots the course will ask you to play. Desert courses and old Donald Ross–designed courses like Pinehurst No. 2 will generally demand a high-lob club in the 60-degree range.

Next, amass a little collection of fairway woods (along with perhaps even one of the popular new driving irons) that range in loft angle from about 14 degrees all the way to 28 or higher. These are your three-, four-, five-, seven-, and nine-woods. Experiment so you know, over time, the approximate carry distance of each club. "If the course you're scheduled to play is tight off the tee," says Poole (who carries a seven-wood for use on only two holes of Chester Valley's 18) "you may end up hitting two or three different lofted woods off the tee. If its par-5s are short, one of those lofted woods may be a valuable go-for-it club with the second shot." If the course is wide open, Poole advises that your bag be stocked with the strongest-lofted metal woods you own.

"Ben Hogan won the U.S. Open at Merion Golf Club in 1950 without a seven-iron in his bag," Poole points out. "He played his practice rounds and determined that he wouldn't need seven-iron anywhere. That allowed him to carry his one-iron, which he used to hit his final, winning shot on number 18—one of the most famous shots in all of golf history." While that sort of destiny may not await the rest of us, we can still, Poole advises, carry the right clubs for the course and conditions that await us.

Equipment Options to Restart the Struggling Golfer

Full-service, professional club fitting is the ideal way to gear yourself up for peak-performance golf. But not every golfer feels quite ready for this scientific approach. Others are open to dynamic fitting but can't find a recommended pro in their area. And then there is the type of golfer who believes that to shake himself out of the doldrums, he has to go into the golf shop and part with a little money. The temporary comfort of having leaped into action will often carry over to the practice range and then to the golf course. Here is a list often recommended by pro instructors:

▶ Whatever your most-lofted fairway wood is, get one with four to seven degrees more loft. In other words, if you carry a seven-wood, get a nine-wood.

▶ Switch to an offset driver or a driver with a "hooked" face angle (especially if you're slicing).

▶ Try (at least in a shop or store) the long putter (especially if you have the yips—but even if you're putting terribly without yipping).

▶ Try a low-profile fairway wood—one with a crown that is barely as high as the golf ball when the club is set at address.

▶ Test out one of the newly marketed "hybrid" driving clubs: It's part wood, part iron, and definitely in vogue.

▶ Get a sand iron with lots of bounce (i.e., downward angle from the leading edge to the trailing edge) and use it only out of the sand, not from the fairway.

▶ Switch to super-distance golf balls (legal ones, that is), especially if short, weak drives are the main plague of your game.

Give Your Putter a Checkup and a Tweak

There is inspiration and lots of sound technical data in Sue Kaffenburgh's putter-fitting advice on page 150, but some golfers like the idea of going years or even decades with one putter. If that's the route you want to go but your putting game isn't cooperating, try the following:

▶ Go to a club repair center and check out its selection of putter grips. These can vary in feel and thickness much more than grips we use on the regular clubs, making a new putter grip your ticket to an entirely new feel on the greens.

▶ Whether you regrip your putter or not, experiment with different swing-weight feels by sticking lead tape lightly on the back of the blade. Don't adhere the tape securely until you've decided if you like the heavier weighting. If you do like the feel of some added head weight, put most of the tape you're going to use toward the heel and toe of the head, then perform a sweet spot test.

▶ The sweet spot test can be done quickly with the help of a wooden golf tee. Pinch the handle of your putter between your club and forefinger and raise the handle high so the head of your putter is at or near eye level. Let the putter swing lightly, and hold the tee horizontal, allowing the face of the putter to contact the sharp end of the tee as though it were a ball. Determine the true sweet spot of your putter by finding the location that, when struck against the tee point, causes extremely little or absolutely no twist of the blade, just a straight rebound. If that spot doesn't line up with the notch marked by the manufacturer to show you where to make contact, erase the original mark and make an accurate one.

▶ Once you have the new spot marked, keep rechecking it as you add any additional lead tape. Make sure to place the tape so that it doesn't cause the sweet spot to move again.

You'll be back in business on the greens, with your trusty but now tuned-up putter confidently in hand.

Chapter 20

Habits and Tricks of the Pros

ID Every Ball to Avoid Delays and Mixups

The penalty for a lost ball is stroke and distance—back to the point you played from, hitting four from the spot where you just had hit your second (or five from where you'd hit your third, etc.). Professional golfers don't lose as many balls as we amateurs do, and not simply because they hit them straighter. On tour, every single ball is identified with a distinctive marking, and that one little habit pays off in savings of time and even a few strokes a season.

To keep track of your ball like a professional, buy an indelible marker and keep it in the ball pocket of your golf bag at all times. Select a unique-looking slash or set of dots as your personal marking, and imprint it with the pen on two opposite poles of every ball you own. When you buy new balls, be in the habit of immediately taking them from their sleeves and marking them with your imprint. Even when you change brands, which most of us do, the imprint will always ID your ball quickly. Playing partners (and golfers wandering from other fairways) will be far less likely to hit your ball accidentally. They may even join in the hunt for your off-line shots more readily, knowing there won't be any uncertainty about whether the ball they find is yours or not. When it's time to get yardages off a sprinkler head, your fellow players will find they give you your yardage first, because they know for sure who to call out the number to.

This tip is a simple, no-skill-required adjustment to your normal golfing habits, but its benefits are manifold, and only appreciable by the player who adopts the practice and sticks by it. If nothing else, it'll make you feel a bit more like a pro.

Learn from Your Warmup and Be Ready to Play

The more golf you play, the more you realize preround warmup can be a lab experiment that reveals how the golfer (that's you) and the golf course are going to interact. During warmup for your next important round, sleuth out answers to the following questions:

▶ Do I feel limber and relaxed? If not (and instead you feel stiff and anxious), think about easing your way around the golf course for the first few holes, hitting less club, laying up, shooting at greens instead of pins.

▶ Which way is my ball tending to curve, and how much is it curving? Whatever the answer, figure on playing shots of that shape all day. You're unlikely to reverse the trend in a preround warmup.

▶ Do I have good feel for distance from 110 yards and in? If the answer is no, this is one part of the game you might be able to sharpen up during the warmup period. Just mind the advice of David Lawrence, who teaches at Brentwood Golf and Country Club in White Lake, Michigan: Don't blindly trust the golf balls on the range. "A lot of them are limited flight but don't have a marking to indicate it," says Lawrence.

▶ On straight, level warmup putts, am I going past, leaving them short, missing right, or missing left? Sports vision expert Dr. Craig Farnsworth says our visual knack of locating objects (like golf holes) in three-dimensional space varies from day to day. If three straight practice putts from eight feet miss to the right, move to another hole, set up an eight-footer and aim six inches left. When that putt goes in, you know you have a slight visual adjustment to make for that day.

▶ Is the ball flying normally today? Even if it's not windy, unusual coolness or the heavy air of summer can affect distance by half a club or more.

▶ How are the greens rolling? The practice putting green may not be a similar speed to the greens on the course. Get a sense of the pace on the practice green, then adjust once on the course.

▶ Any local rules in force? If preferred lies are being allowed, be sure to take advantage. Likewise with any "leaf rules," ground under repair, and temporary green situations.

Be Sure to Exploit Your Home Field Advantage

The everyday sports-psychology practice of tour-pro adviser Patrick Cohn puts him in close contact with men and women who are nakedly lustful of low-scoring rounds. Cohn works morning to night trying to help these birdie-greedy players put up 67s and 65s. Aware that we regular golfers are only mildly starved for low scores, Cohn spares us the heavy psychological artillery. But he does insist we use one scoring edge: the "home field" advantage.

"It only makes sense that you go for your career round on the course you know best," says Cohn, "if for no other reason than that you know the speed of the greens and which way the putts break." If local knowledge of the greens offers a two- or three-stroke edge over what you could score with similar ball-striking on a comparable course you are unfamiliar with, then that's just a start.

"A personal-best, career-low round is most likely to happen on a day when you devise a hole-by-hole game plan and execute it," says Cohn. "You'd be hard-pressed to do that on a course you don't know, but on your home field you could indeed plan your work and work your plan." Specifically he is talking about where to hit three-wood, where to go for a par-5 in two, where to hold back, and where to take a brave line to the hole.

"Overall, you can be freer in your play on a course you know intimately," Cohn says. "Of course, the disadvantage is that you know where the trouble is, and you remember all the times you hit into it." Those of you with 80-breaking as a current obsession didn't hear that last comment.

Play Your "A" Game Despite the Company

We've all heard the complaint of a fellow golfer that he "couldn't play a lick today because of that damn Charlie." The

Charlie in question might have played too slow, played too fast, talked too much, or laughed too loud. When it's time to compete in a match or a tournament, the advice of former PGA Professional of the Year Tom Addis is to look inward, look outward, look anywhere but at the human distraction that might throw you off your game.

"In golf, there is always somewhere else to focus your attention besides the fellow player you're not compatible with," explains Addis, a teaching pro turned golf-management consultant. For golfers who suffer from "rabbit ears" during serious rounds, he offers the following advice:

▶ Take cues from those who can and those who can't tune out the bothersome talker or whistler. "Look at David Duval, Tiger Woods, or Annika Sorenstam," he says. "They aren't just hitting great shots, they've also developed an unshakeable focus. It shows on their faces and in the way they move. Then look at the junior level, where you've got a lot of talent but the focus isn't there yet. The young player hasn't found a way to keep people around from breaking his concentration." So when Charlie gets up to his irritating tricks, emulate the top pros, not the raw youngsters.

▶ When the pace is slow, turn the course into a nature trail. "There are places in golf that are so beautiful, they're said to make it hard to focus on the shots you have to play," says Addis. "I say work that to your advantage. When the pace of play is satisfactory to you, take in that beauty in glimpses. When it's so slow as to be a distraction, spend more time observing the scenery and seeing it in detail."

▶ Make the round with troublesome Charlie your best "visualization" round of the year. "We could all do a lot more visualizing of how our shots should fly and land than we actually do," says Addis. "The best possible way to block out distractions is to really see the ball flying, landing, and rolling just the way you want it to."

Fight Fatigue (Physical and Mental) and Finish That Round

The lament of golfers who "played well on the front nine, then blew up on the back" is all too familiar to teaching pro David Lawrence, who is based at Brentwood Golf and Country Club in scenic White Lake, Michigan. Lawrence's first piece of advice for players whose opening nine routinely seems sharper and lower-scoring than their back is to assess the fatigue factor. Did you rush more shots? Lose concentration? Hit without knowing the hazards ahead of you? Fail to read each putt, even when you had plenty of time?

"One question I always ask," says Lawrence, "is whether they got angry or visibly upset on that back nine. That's a sign of fatigue, because you need energy to keep your emotions together. When somebody throws a club, for example, that's usually a sign of extreme fatigue," he says. Keep the weary-golf blues away by following Lawrence's five basic steps.

1. Stretch before you play. "The average golfer's minute or two of stretching is totally insufficient," says Lawrence. "It works for about three swings. Staying sharp requires full blood flow, and to get that you need a half-hour of

stretching. Do it at home, watching the sports high-lights, and stretch the entire body."

2. Eat the right foods. "Fruits, juices, and a light breakfast or lunch will keep your energy from being diverted from golf and spent on digestion," he says. An apple should be your quick energy food, a banana gives you extended energy. Keep them in your golf bag and don't worry if they get a little warm.

3. Hydrate constantly. "If you actually feel thirsty, it's too late—you've already stressed your body. Drink water as a habit, not a response to thirst."

4. Practice thinking. "Much of your energy in a round of golf goes to analyzing and preparing. Whenever you practice or warm up, short game or long game," he advises. "Make sure you're thinking about targets, yardage, putt speed . . . all the considerations you'll need to make during the round."

5. Manage expectations. "I've seen golfers go from play-ing their home course, which might have a slope rat-ing of 130 and where their normal round is 85 or 88, to a resort course that might have a slope of 120," says Lawrence. "They head to the tee thinking 'I'm going to break 80 today.' That's a mistake, and a real recipe for mental fatigue." Play solid golf in those situations, is Lawrence's advice, and let the score happen.

David Lawrence's expert professional advice is available at no charge to golfers who e-mail him at daveL02@yahoo.com.

Compete at Your Best with a Pre-Round Routine

PGA Tour superstar Lee Trevino was renowned for his attention to detail and steady habits leading up to any competitive round of golf. He summed up the value of his organized approach in an honest comment: "On a given day, I may not be able to outplay and out-putt everybody else in the field—that's beyond my control. But I do know that I can out-prepare everybody else."

The same can easily go for any of us average golfers playing in the company tournament or the fall fourball at our local club. If we followed Trevino's sage advice, we would do as follows:

1. Check and recheck all equipment the night before: Clean trash out of the bag; put in sunscreen and water bottles; ID any new golf balls; check shoes for worn laces or faulty spikes.

2. Be certain of directions and travel time: Build in a cushion for unforeseen delays en route. Double-check your starting time and write it on a sheet of paper with any other reminders you're giving yourself.

3. Plan what and when you are going to eat. Stock a small cooler with juices, fruit, and possibly a sandwich.

4. Set a schedule for morning stretching at home. Forty minutes on the carpet, limbering up legs, torso, shoulders, neck, and so on, are generally needed if you want to be at your best.

5. Budget your warmup time and follow the schedule you set, from the short-game area to the full range. Set aside time for asking about the course setup and looking over pin sheets and yardage guides.
6. Build in some extra time for relaxation at the course. Bring a newspaper or a magazine to read for thirty minutes on a bench or in the grill room. This can be as important a mood setter as anything else you do to prepare for competition.

And naturally, be sure to get enough sleep the night before. But if you go to bed knowing you are this ready to compete, sleep should come easy.